To the Winds Our Sails

Irish Writers Translate Galician Poetry

Edited by

MARY O'DONNELL AND MANUELA PALACIOS

salmonpoetry

Published in 2010 by
Salmon Poetry
Cliffs of Moher, County Clare, Ireland
Website: www.salmonpoetry.com
Email: info@salmonpoetry.com

ISBN 978-1-907056-37-6

Cover artwork: Mosaic © Arcobaleno | Dreamstime.com
Typesetting & Design: Siobhán Hutson

Published with financial assistance from the Arts Council

Remembering languages no longer spoken, and languages not yet born, this book is dedicated to those who attempt to keep the flow of words and experience alive.

Contents

Acknowledgements 12
Introduction by Mary O'Donnell 15
Galician Women Poets Today: Moving from Strength to Strength
  by Manuela Palacios 21

Luz Pozo Garza

Os palacios de inverno 30
Benvida a "San Felicísimo" 32
Bosque de rododendros 34
Páxina Atlántica 38
Avalon Avalon 40

María do Carme Kruckenberg

Falemos das acusacións incorrectas… 46
Non sei como fun pisando… 48
O cristal axústase… 50
Lembro aqueles tempos do verán… 52
Recordas como ladraba… 54

Xohana Torres

Penélope 58
Ofelia 60
Sibila en Ribadavia 62
Chámome imaxe á malva luz da hora. Ás veces vén
  a néboa que me muda de todo 64
Sempre baixaba pola Praza Vella… 66

Contents

Acknowledgements   12
Introduction by Mary O'Donnell   15
Galician Women Poets Today: Moving from Strength to Strength
    by Manuela Palacios   21

Luz Pozo Garza   by **Nuala Ní Dhomhnaill**

    Winter Palaces   31
    Welcome to 'San Felicísimo'   33
    Forest of Rhododendrons   35
    Page of the Atlantic   39
    Avalon Avalon   41

María do Carme Kruckenberg
    by **Anne Le Marquand Hartigan**
    Let's Talk about False Accusations...   47
    Ní Aithním mo Choischéim Fhéin... by **Rita Kelly**   49
    The Mirror Reflects...   51
    I Remember Those Summer Days...   53
    Do You Remember How the Dog...   55

Xohana Torres   by **Celia de Fréine**

    Penelope   59
    Ophelia   61
    Sybil in Ribadavia   63
    My Name Is Image in the Hour's Mauve Light.
        At Times the Fog That Transforms Me Descends   65
    Many's the Time I'd Wend My Way through
        the Old Square...   67

Marilar Aleixandre

derrotas domésticas   72
o diario (3 rabuda)   74
varrer as cinzas   76
luis   78
comedores de cabezas   80

Luz Pichel

Poema prólogo   84
Queimar a leña   86
Pésanlle as pólas á figueira coa carga dos figos   88
Non se sabe case nada   90
Sachando na horta   92

Chus Pato

PORQUE NON É SÓ O IDIOMA O QUE ESTÁ
    AMEAZADO...   96
A voz era pánico...   98
Un cabalo para as musas   102

Ana Romaní

Os lagartos vírona pasar...   108
Por que sei que te vas ás veces...   110
Fuga   112
Que os cachalotes me suban polas pernas...   114
No medio da praza...   116

Marilar Aleixandre   by **Mary O'Malley**

domestic defeats   73
the diary (3 surly)   75
sweeping up the ashes   77
luis, by **Martin Nugent**   79
the head eaters   81

Luz Pichel   by **Catherine Phil MacCarthy**

Prologue Poem   85
Burning the Firewood   87
The Branches of the Fig Tree Are Laden
    with Its Crop of Figs   89
Almost Nothing Is Known   91
Ag Grafadh san Úllord   93

Chus Pato   by **Lorna Shaughnessy**

BECAUSE IT IS NOT ONLY LANGUAGE THAT IS
    THREATENED ...   97
The Voice was Pure Panic...   99
Capall do na mBéithe   103
    by **Lorna Shaughnessy with Rita Kelly**

Ana Romaní   by **Maurice Harmon**

The Lizards Watched Her As She Passed...   109
Because I know You Sometimes Leave...   111
Escape   113
Would That the Sperm Whales Would
    Climb My Legs...   115
Lar na Cearnóige   117

María do Cebreiro

A memoria é o espazo da reapropiación...   120
A Terra Devastada   122
Lúa   124
X.   128
The Death of Lieutenant General Sir Moore. 1809 130

María Lado

un   136
tres   138
sete   140
cuqui   142
catro   144

Xiana Arias

Este é o lugar onde medra a morte...   148
Non hai pistolas...   150
Recoñézome na dor...   152
Sentada na porta da casa...   154
Isto non é literatura feminina...   156

About the Poets
  by María Xesús Nogueira and Laura Lojo   159

About the Editors   168

María do Cebreiro   by **Caitríona O'Reilly**

Memory Is a Circumscribed Space...   121
The Waste Land   123
Moon   125
X.   129
The Death of Lieutenant General Sir Moore. 1809   131

María Lado   by **Máighréad Medbh**

one   137
three   139
seven   141
cuqui, by **Rita Kelly**   143
four   145

Xiana Arias   by **Paddy Bushe**

Here Is the Place of Death's Growing...   149
There Are No Guns...   151
Aithním mé Féin sa bhFulaingt...   153
By the Door of Her House, Sitting...   155
This Is Not Feminine Literature...   157

About the Poets
by María Xesús Nogueira and Laura Lojo   159

About the Editors   168

Acknowledgements

The editors wish to acknowledge the support of the following institutions:

The Spanish MINISTERIO DE CIENCIA E INNOVACIÓN, and the CONSELLERÍA DE ECONOMÍA E INDUSTRIA, XUNTA DE GALICIA, which have funded our projects on contemporary Irish and Galician women writers (Refs. FFI2008-02401E/FILO, FFI2009-08475/FILO, INCITE09- 204127PR, and finally INCITE09-ENA204035ES for the research network *Discourse and Identity*).

The ASOCIACIÓN DE ESCRITORES EN LINGUA GALEGA (AELG) for their financial support and logistic facililities.

The INSTITUTO CERVANTES, Dublin, and its director Dr. Julia Piera, for generous interest and assistance in this project.

***

The editors and the publisher, Salmon Poetry, gratefully acknowledge permission, from the authors and publishers below, to translate into English and Irish and to reprint, in this anthology, poems which appeared formerly in the following collections:

Luz Pozo Garza, *As arpas de Iwerddon*. Ourense: Ediciones Linteo, 2005.

María do Carme Kruckenberg, *As complexas mareas da noite*. A Coruña: Espiral Maior, 2006.

María do Carme Kruckenberg, *Os límites do arreguizo*. A Coruña: Espiral Maior, 2008.

Xohana Torres, *Poesía reunida (1957-2001)*. [It contains the collections *Tempo de ría* (Espiral Maior, 1992) and *Estacións ao mar* (Galaxia, 1980)]. Ed. Luciano Rodríguez. Santiago: P. E.N. Clube de Galicia / Editorial Danú, 2004.

Marilar Aleixandre, *Catálogo de velenos*. Ferrol: Sociedade de Cultura Valle-Inclán/ Fundación Caixa Galicia, 1999. Esquío Poetry Prize.

Marilar Aleixandre, *Desmentindo a primavera*. Vigo: Xerais, 2003.

Marilar Aleixandre, *Abecedario de árbores*. Santiago: Concellaría de Cultura, Concello de Santiago/ Editorial Compostela S.A., 2006.

Marilar Aleixandre, *Mudanzas*. Santiago: P.E.N. Clube de Galicia/Editorial Danú, 2007. V Caixanova Poetry Prize.

Luz Pichel, *Casa pechada*. Ferrol: Sociedad de Cultura Valle Inclán/Fundación Caixa Galicia, 2006. XXVI Esquío Poetry Prize.

Chus Pato, *m-Talá*. Vigo: Xerais, 2000. [Also translated into English by Erín Moure. 58, Velwell Road, Exeter: Shearsman, 2009].

Chus Pato, *Hordas de escritura*. Vigo: Xerais, 2008. Spanish Critics' Prize.

Chus Pato, "Un cabalo para as musas" (unpublished).

Ana Romaní, *Das últimas mareas*. A Coruña: Espiral Maior, 1994.

Ana Romaní, *Arden*. A Coruña: Espiral Maior, 1998.

Ana Romaní, *Love me tender. 24 pezas mínimas para unha caixa de música*. Santiago: Concellaría de Cultura, Concello de Santiago/Editorial Compostela S.A., 2005.

María do Cebreiro, *o estadio do espello*. Vigo: Xerais, 1998.

María do Cebreiro, *Non queres que o poema te coñeza*. Santiago: P. E.N. Clube de Galicia/Editorial Danú, 2004. II Caixanova Poetry Prize.

María do Cebreiro, *Os hemisferios*. Vigo: Galaxia, 2006.

María do Cebreiro, *Cuarto de outono*. Santiago: Sotelo Blanco, 2008.

María do Cebreiro, "THE DEATH OF LIEUTENANT GENERAL SIR JOHN MOORE 1809". *Poemas históricos* (unpublished).

María Lado, *casa atlántica, casa cabaret*. Vigo: Xerais, 2001.

María Lado, *berlín*. Santiago: Concellaría de Cultura, Concello de Santiago/ Editorial Compostela S.A., 2005.

María Lado, *nove*. A Estrada: Edicións Fervenza, 2008. Avelina Valladares Prize.

Xiana Arias, *Ortigas*. A Coruña: Espiral Maior, 2007. XIX National Prize Xosé María Pérez Parallé.

Xiana Arias, "Este é o lugar onde medra a morte". From "Cleo de dez a doce", published in *Pirata*. Santiago: Brigadas de Intervención Rápida George Grosz in support of Cineclube Compostela, 2007.

Xiana Arias, *Acusación*. Vigo: Galaxia, 2009.

13

Introduction

by MARY O'DONNELL

In recent decades, Irish poets have been accustomed to being the focus of literary research and scholarship from abroad. It has become an almost unquestioned aspect of being an Irish writer, and the work of a significant number has been translated to other languages, analysed, researched and/or the subject of literary conferences and summer schools the length and breadth of Europe, not to mention the all-welcoming, parental interest of universities, colleges and institutions in the United States. To be an Irish writer has often meant that our concerns became the scholarly concerns of others, that our lines and paragraphs were open to interpretation world-wide, our issues, themes, narratives and socio-cultural insights the material for academic investment and dialogue. One could argue that we have been pampered by such attention, and indeed until recently that appeared to be the prevailing response in our greater island neighbour across the Irish Sea, where finally a kind of *Sonnenuntergang* regarding Irish writers and prizes, Irish writers and favourable comment seems partially underway.

In this context, it struck me after a visit to Santiago de Compostela in summer 2006, that there was a dearth of information and interest in Ireland regarding Galician poets. My awareness had been stirred almost imperceptibly. The purpose of my visit had been to give a lecture on the journey from imagination to print for Irish women writers from the 1980s to the present. It was a sultry, humid few days during which I wandered the city, absorbing something that initially I could not quite identify. There was a sense of something being out of kilter, and yet something falling rightly into place. Threads of a recognisable music caught me off-guard—pure Celtic, wavering on the air from some of the shops, or rattling the guts of the casual passer-by wherever young people played beneath shaded, ancient archways as the reverberations of what I could only call *bodhrán* and *uilleann pipes* followed me everywhere.

Then there were the images—simple, recognisable—Celtic knots, circles, trees and triads, in jewellery and shop signs, wherever the casual visitor might wander. There was a sense that, in Galicia, Celticism—the easily digested *tourist* brand that includes silver, tea-towels and CDs—was alive and well in a manner easily matched by any Irish town or in the summer throng of Dublin's Nassau Street.

Out of these impressions and further reading, one year later the idea for this anthology was born, and at the time it seemed relatively uncomplicated. Thanks to the enthusiastic response from my co-editor and collaborator Manuela Palacios in Santiago and also, significantly, from Jessie Lendennie of Salmon Poetry in Co. Clare, things slid into place very quickly at first and the decision to proceed was made. It was then a matter of securing our poets —on both sides of the equation— and inviting them to participate in this project.

I read more about Galicia and Celticism. As I suspected, sceptical arguments have also been mounted regarding alleged Celtic roots in Galicia and an ancient co-Celtic, utopian brother and sisterhood. Galicia and Ireland have traditionally shared various other social circumstances that have characterised their identity. Both have been strongholds of Catholicism in Europe and—despite declining religious observance, (and the current rupture in the Irish church, itself a cause of ongoing investigation)—Catholic morality continues to be decisive in family and sexual politics for significant numbers of people.

Both communities have two official languages, Irish and English in Ireland, whereas in Galicia they have the vernacular and Spanish. Both English and Spanish are traditionally viewed by many as having been imposed on two communities which already had complete and developed languages, themselves a naturally evolved repository of considerable enriching historical, mythic and social inheritance. Admittedly, attitudes towards the languages vary and some differences apply: Irish and English are linguistically much further apart than Galician and Spanish (both derived from Latin), and Galician is much more widely spoken than Irish is today. Is there a danger that notwithstanding the fluency of some three million Galicians, the language of both our communities may eventually disappear off the fragile linguistic world map and remain—as it so often does in Ireland—as a sanctified code to be pulled out and dressed up on official and formal occasions?

Another difference is an environmental one. The oil tanker *Prestige* split in two in November 2002 releasing millions of gallons of oil along the wildlife-rich Galician coastline. There exists a more heightened consciousness of the fragile nature of the eco-system than in Ireland, and some of its literary writers have engaged with this aspect of connection to landscape.

Yet what became apparent was the amount and quality of articles, books and pamphlets which demonstrated a categorically clear interest in *Irish* writers *by* Galician scholars and poets over the years. The interest from there to here has been unstinting. Whether or not one argues that the Celtic link between our two countries is real or idealised is, in a way, very much beside the point. The evidence of a need to connect with a culture Galicia dreamed of, both fact and imagining, was evident.

Further back Galicia's interest in Ireland had peaked several times, especially during the second half of the nineteenth century, with writers Eduardo Pondal and Manuel Murguía. The latter based his *Galicia* and his *Historia de Galicia* in a regionally-oriented Celticism and in a romantic ideology which were of literary and cultural importance. One of the outstanding figures of his time, Murguía's marriage to the iconic poet Rosalía de Castro, and his friendship with Manuel Curros Enríquez were significant, to the extent that his Celticist ideals gave rise to a group based in A Coruña called "A Cova Céltica"

[The Celtic Lair]. Galicia's literary and cultural revival peaked earlier than that of Ireland, but a resurgence again followed in the 1920s, and in 1926 the first translation of fragments of James Joyce's *Ulysses* was rendered into Galician by Otero Pedrayo. Today, many researchers in the three Galician universities are working on Irish studies.

★★★

By proceeding chronologically through this volume it is possible to discern a trail of interests, issues and concerns in the work of these Galician poets (outlined by Manuela Palacios in her introductory essay). In a sense, it can be read as unfolding in three movements, and this division is reflected in the selection of the Irish poets. Thus one of our greatest poets, Nuala Ní Dhomhnaill, translates the myth-enriched and explorative vitality of Luz Pozo Garza; Anne Le Marquand Hartigan, Celia de Fréine, Mary O'Malley, Catherine Phil MacCarthy, Lorna Shaughnessy, Maurice Harmon, Caitríona O'Reilly, Máighréad Medbh, and Paddy Bushe follow on a trail of discourse which embraces political struggle and identity, feminism, literary tradition and the interrogation of these subjects. Each Irish poet is, in their own lives, distinguished by differing approaches to technique, thematic schema and vision, but all are imbued with an ear for the music of language.

Aided initially by the indispensable work of Minia Bongiorno García, who provided the cribs which enabled the Irish writers to create their versions, it was decided that of the five poems contributed by each Galician writer, one of these was to be rendered to Irish—a minimal way, perhaps, of acknowledging the still living presence and identity of our original cultural language. Six of the Irish writers selected are Irish speakers, and for those who are not, the bilingual writer-poet, linguist and scholar Rita Kelly secured the Irish translations, with one from Martin Nugent.

Styles and interpretations vary from the literal to the re-imagining of certain poems. Several of the Galician poets expressed willingness to having their poems freely explored in these versions. Therefore, in some instances, literalism is not necessarily to the fore. It remains one of the essential questions whenever translation is in the air: how should it be done—an attempt at a literal transposition, an attempt to capture the *spirit* of the poem, regardless what gymnastics of language and phrasing, or is it a bit like making a dog stand on its hind legs? In other words, can it be done at all?

As so often in translation, it remains a matter of discernment, personal approach and—sometimes—political strategy (conscious and unconscious) on the translator's part. The translator needs, ideally, to find some sense of the originator's identity with which s/he can uncover a linguistic resonance in the host language. There is also, then, the matter of cultural identity itself, and the translator's understanding of it. As Prof. Michael Cronin, Director of the Centre for Translation and Textual Studies at Dublin City University, remarks in the opening page of his work *Translation and Identity* (Routledge, 2006), "identity is one of the most important political and cultural issues of our time", and in this context he examines the manner in which translation has played a critical role in shaping discourse "around identity, language and cultural survival in the past and in the present".

With this in mind, this anthology hopes to contribute to the further shaping of such discourse, given the commonality of socio-cultural and to some degree, political histories, shared by Ireland and Galicia. It is hoped that in Galicia the work of the Irish poets will be seen as a reciprocation, an unequivocal answering-call to the sometimes visionary work of our sister-poets further down the Atlantic seaboard as they too wrestle with diverse challenges—each to her own time—and that finally it can be said that in literary terms a two-way channel between our cultures has been forged.

My thanks to the Galician poets who contributed poems to the project. Without them nothing would have happened. Thanks and admiration also to the Irish poets who engaged with them, sometimes for months on end, who have lived with the poems and made decisions regarding best choices, line-breaks, punctuation, interpretation, revising them often, deeply involved in an enterprise the aim of which throughout has been to do justice to the poems made by the women of Galicia.

In a time when the local and the global are so often interchangeable as concepts, when cosmopolitanism can be viewed as surging uprootedness instead of something which indicates evolving *exchange* and *mutual dialogue*, it seems vital now to make steps towards the latter brand of cosmopolitanism, remembering what it has emerged from in this case—two histories of struggle, two histories almost assimilated by greater, eloquent cultures that communicate in what are decisively termed *world* languages (meaning incontestable language presence).

Thanks to the advances of technology, the world may be a village as a village is the world, but that does not automatically signify an absence of connectedness. On the contrary, we find ourselves in the contemporary world at a nexus of heightened awareness of what is *other* and *same* and the ability to recognise both, in this instance especially, in the inter-webbing of the cultures of Galicia and Ireland.

MARY O'DONNELL
Dublin 2010

Galician Women Poets Today: Moving from Strength to Strength

by MANUELA PALACIOS

In the last three decades, Galician literature has experienced a radical transformation which has undoubtedly benefited from the cultural and linguistic policies furthered by the 1981 Galician Statute of Autonomy. Fran Alonso, assistant director of Edicións Xerais, provides us with some revealing figures: "the total of 68 titles published in Galician and Castilian in 1975 rises to 1,665 books published in the Galician language in 2006" (2010: 37). At present, when we speak of Galician literature, we usually mean writing in the Galician language, since a majority of Galician writers have chosen the vernacular as their means of artistic expression. The conspicuous growth of the publishing industry has certainly been favoured by the economic prosperity of recent decades, which has allowed some substantial public funding for the advancement of Galician culture.

In this dynamic cultural context, poetry has been a cherished genre, in part because of its roots in the prestigious Galician-Portuguese secular and religious lyric which reached its zenith in the thirteenth century—the *Cantigas* that Nuala Ní Dhomhnaill relishes in her poem "Ceol" (1999). The Galician literary revival in the second half of the nineteenth century had a woman poet as its figurehead, Rosalía de Castro (1837-1885), who—for better or worse—has been appropriated as an icon of national identity. As the poet Chus Pato suggests, Galician women poets today need to renegotiate their pact with this literary foremother on new conditions that may let the daughters breathe (2008b: 128).

Since Rosalía's times, other women writers have worked vigorously for the advance of Galician poetry, and this anthology includes writers such as Luz Pozo Garza, María do Carme Kruckenberg and Xohana Torres, who began publishing in the 1950s—in the extremely hostile conditions of General Franco's dictatorship. A second wave of writers, influenced to various degrees by feminist discourses, the struggle for democracy and Galician national identity in the 1970s, is also represented in this anthology by Marilar Aleixandre, Luz Pichel, Chus Pato and Ana Romaní—even if, interestingly enough, many of these writers did not start publishing book-length collections until the late 1980s and early 1990s. Finally, a younger generation of women poets has elbowed its way into the literary establishment, while their poetry calls into question deep-rooted assumptions about national literature, literary tradition and women's writing. María do Cebreiro, María Lado and Xiana Arias are three among this prolific group of emerging writers. It is our good fortune that these three generations often work side by side, inspire one another and join forces to advance the presence of women in the public sphere of literature.

Luz Pozo Garza's poems, from her collection *As arpas de Iwerddon* [The Harps of Iwerddon] (2005), bear witness to the vitality of Celticism in contemporary poetry. The *Lebor Gabála Éren* or *Book of Invasions of Ireland* suggests a possible connection between Galicia and Ireland through the myth of the sons of Mil and their poet Amergin—the great-grandson of Breogán, the mythical father of the Galician nation. However, Luz Pozo Garza shifts the stress from the account of the invasion to that of the amorous fusion between the mother's Galician culture and the daughter's adopted Irish traditions. Very much like Nuala Ní Dhomhnaill, Pozo has past myths inform the daily reality of the modern world in verse that proceeds with the grace and poise of a classic writer.

María do Carme Kruckenberg's poems from her two collections *As complexas mareas da noite* [The Complex Tides of the Night] (2006) and *Os límites do arreguizo* [Shiver's Limits] (2008) entwine critical scrutiny of the present with memories of a life lived to the full. Like Anne Hartigan's poetry,

Kruckenberg's vindicates love and pleasure, but she does so from a sober stance which simultaneously explores the tensions between lexicon and rhythm. Our triad of doyennes of Galician poetry is completed with Xohana Torres, whose poetry resounds in that of many contemporaries; such is her mastery. Torres' Penelope, in the eponymous poem, refuses the domestic and expectant role ascribed to her in Homer's *Odyssey* and claims the ocean as the metaphorical space into which women must venture. It comes as no surprise, then, that many Galician and Irish women writers are intent on postulating new odysseys, as Celia de Fréine's *imram/odyssey* (2010) also attests. Apart from rewriting Western literary classics, Torres' collections *Estacións ao mar* [Seasons to the Sea] (1980) and *Tempo de ría* [Estuary Time] (1992) delve into those spaces and people that once acted as havens of innocence, though the sense of loss is always kept in check by the poet's sophisticated craft.

Marilar Aleixandre's poems from *Catálogo de velenos* [Catalogue of Poisons] (1999) and *Desmentindo a primavera* [Denying Spring] (2003) elaborate on the struggle between patriarchal injunctions and expectations—even if these are sometimes perpetuated by women themselves—and a young woman's craving for freedom. The undisguised affection and admiration felt for the father and mother figures collides with the lyric subject's necessity to live life according to her own convictions. From *Abecedario de árbores* [ABC of Trees] (2006), "luis" revels in those Celtic legends which continue to inspire Galician poetry and strengthen the ties between Galicia and Ireland, while her most recent collection *Mudanzas* [Shiftings] (2007) rewrites Ovid's *Metamorphoses* by purveying a much-needed woman-centred gaze.

Luz Pichel, a member of the Galician diaspora in Madrid, has written both in Spanish and Galician, and her poetic interests range from present-day metropolitan life to memories of a rural childhood. *Casa pechada* [Locked House] (2006) invests the rural world with a surrealist perspective that is not uncommon in either Galician or Irish folk culture. There is no room for the picturesque in this poetry which constitutes a truthful reconstruction not only of the pain and hardships but also of the pleasures and affections experienced in childhood, as they are remembered by a woman who returns to her village in order to lock up her parents' house for good. Each of Pichel's poems defies predictability and unsettles our preconceptions about country life.

Chus Pato is a notable representative of the engaged poet, as she is deeply committed to critique capitalist commodification of language, literature and human life in general. Although her book *m-Talá* (2000) calls into question the transparency of language and poets' capacity to convey their messages—thereby demanding a very participative reader—Pato's writing perseveres in the defence of justice. She tests the limits of what can be said in poetry by challenging genre boundaries and defamiliarising the reading process in an act of resistance to literary conventions that domesticate our intellect. *In Hordas de escritura* [Hordes of Writing] (2008a), Pato deploys a multiplicity of voices from different contexts and times, thus showing that poetry equals excess. Rather than fit the world into the poem, she has it erupt from the lines like lava.

Ana Romaní's collection *Love me tender. 24 pezas mínimas para unha caixa de música* [24 Minimal Pieces for a Music Box] (2005) has its genesis in a piece of journal news: between 30% and 50% of women in the world are beaten and humiliated by their male partners. These poems expose the traps of that kind of amorous discourse which relies on possessiveness, dominance, control, poor self-esteem and submission; that is to say, what Maurice Harmon very aptly calls "love's ferocious intricacy" in his poem "The Winding Stair" (2008). In contrast with this, Romaní's other poems from *Arden* [Blazing] (1998) put forward some empowering and self-assertive feminine models such as those conjured up by awesome and adventurous whales.

The poems by María do Cebreiro included in this anthology give us a fair idea of the wide range of forms and themes that this young poet has already covered. Her first collection, *o estadio do espello* [The Mirror Stage] (1998) starts what will become, in her poetry, a recurrent concern with the creative process, poetic inspiration, the speaking voice, the reader's expectations and literary tradition. *Non queres que o poema te coñeza* [You Don't Want the Poem to Know You] (2004) playfully hides the lyric "I" in a mesh of references to other writers such as, among others, T.S. Eliot, Virginia Woolf and Seamus Heaney. This self-effacing process culminates in the dramatic poems from *Os hemisferios* [The Hemispheres] (2006), which eclipse the authorial voice and represent the characters' tenacious gropings for communication no matter how elusive the latter may turn out to be.

María Lado has won her readers' favour with her appealing performances—a characteristic she shares with her translator in this anthology, Máighréad Medbh—and her experimentation with audiovisual technology. Her poetry spans from an apparent childlike gaze in *casa atlántica, casa cabaret* [atlantic house, cabaret house] (2001) and a deliberate fantasy of idealised love in *berlín* (2005) to the bitter dystopia of *nove* [nine] (2008), a collection marked by the traumatic oil spillage of the tanker Prestige in November 2002 off the Galician coast. Much more formidable than the hostile sea which swallows fishermen and ships or the island that imprisons its inhabitants is the islanders' incapacity to remember. It is for this reason that Lado closes her collection *nove* with a reference to the Prestige oil spillage: so that readers may not forget.

Xiana Arias closes this anthology with poems that sting and accuse us. Her collection *Ortigas* [Stinging Nettles] (2007) denounces violence against women in all its modalities, child abuse, and the marginalisation of disempowered groups with verse that is itself wounded. *Acusación* [Accusation] (2009) interpellates our conscience—often full of good intentions—for our inability to take action, and does so with lucid lines not exempt from acrimonious humour. One perceives in the characters that inhabit these poems a yearning to escape from claustrophobic spaces and oppressive social structures, although they are often too knocked about by life to find the exit.

The writers in this collection display heterogeneous aesthetic approaches and interests, they belong to different generations and have gone through unlike life experiences, though they have one thing in common: their determination to play an active role in the advancement and remodelling of a poetic tradition that cannot afford to do without women's voices. Our anthology wishes to recognise the contribution made by Galician women writers—those who are represented here and many others who would deserve to be—towards the consolidation of Galician-language poetry. This, borrowing Xiana Arias's phrasing in her last poem, may not be *feminine* literature, but it is indeed the writing of women who "score the asphalt with their toenails".

MANUELA PALACIOS
Santiago de Compostela, 2010

WORKS CITED

Aleixandre, Marilar (1999) *Catálogo de velenos.* Ferrol: Sociedad de Cultura Valle-Inclán/ Fundación Caixa Galicia.

———— (2003) *Desmentindo a primavera.* Vigo: Xerais.

———— (2006) *Abecedario de árbores.* Santiago: Concellaría de Cultura, Concello de Santiago/ Editorial Compostela S.A.

———— (2007) *Mudanzas.* Santiago: P.E.N. Clube de Galicia/ Editorial Danú.

Alonso, Fran (2010) "Women, Poetry, and Publishing". *Creation, Publishing, and Criticism. The Advance of Women's Writing.* Eds. María Xesús Nogueira, Laura Lojo and Manuela Palacios. New York: Peter Lang. 35-39.

Arias, Xiana (2007) *Ortigas.* A Coruña: Espiral Maior.

———— (2009) *Acusación.* Vigo: Galaxia.

De Fréine, Celia (2010) *imram/odyssey.* Gaillimh: Arlen House.

Harmon, Maurice (2008) "The Winding Stair". *The Mischievous Boy and Other Poems.* Cliffs of Moher, Co. Clare: Salmon Publishing. 33.

Kruckenberg, María do Carme (2006) *As complexas mareas da noite.* A Coruña: Espiral Maior.

———— (2008) *Os límites do arreguizo.* A Coruña: Espiral Maior.

Lado, María (2001) *casa atlántica, casa cabaret.* Vigo: Xerais.

———— (2005) *berlín.* Santiago: Concellaría de Cultura, Concello de Santiago/ Editorial Compostela S.A.

———— (2008) *nove.* A Estrada: Edicións Fervenza.

María do Cebreiro (1998) *o estadio do espello.* Vigo: Xerais.

———— (2004) *Non queres que o poema te coñeza*. Santiago: P.E.N. Clube de Galicia/Editorial Danú.

———— (2006) *Os hemisferios*. Vigo: Galaxia.

Ní Dhomhnaill, Nuala (1999) "Ceol". *The Water Horse*. Oldcastle: The Gallery Press. 90.

Pato, Chus (2000) *m-Talá*. Vigo: Xerais.

———— (2008a) *Hordas de escritura*. Vigo: Xerais.

———— (2008b) Interview with María Xesús Nogueira in "Los signos de la diferencia. Entrevistas con las poetas Chus Pato y Ana Romaní". *Palabras extremas: Escritoras gallegas e irlandesas de hoy*. Eds. Manuela Palacios and Helena González. A Coruña: Netbiblo. 127-139.

Pichel, Luz (2006) *Casa pechada*. Ferrol: Sociedad de Cultura Valle Inclán/ Fundación Caixa Galicia.

Pozo Garza, Luz (2005) *As arpas de Iwerddon*. Ourense: Linteo.

Romaní, Ana (1998) *Arden*. A Coruña: Espiral Maior.

———— (2005) *Love me tender. 24 pezas mínimas para unha caixa de música*. Santiago: Concellaría de Cultura, Concello de Santiago/ Editorial Compostela S.A.

Torres, Xohana (1980) *Estacións ao mar*. Vigo: Galaxia.

———— (1992) *Tempo de ría*. A Coruña: Espiral Maior.

LUZ POZO GARZA

and

NUALA NÍ DHOMHNAILL

Os palacios de inverno

E todo se cumpría naquela primavera
de auganeve en Dublín

Crucei a luz aínda furtiva
cunha Biblia datada en Compostela
e leveina no colo como un neno durmido
desde a patria

Riba das nubes
a harmonía da luz entraba en alba

Estábase a escribir a vida nunha páxina nova

E lin na nosa lingua os salmos que regulan a alianza
dunha linaxe celta en dúas ribeiras
na igrexa
naquela primavera de auganeve en Dublín

E lin versículo a versículo:
            Entra con todo o honor dunha princesa
            nos palacios do inverno
Non esquezas a patria

As arpas de Iwerddon (2005)

Winter Palaces

And all that was to happen
came to pass that sleety spring in Dublin.

I crossed the quiet, fugitive, light
with a Bible dated in Compostela
that I took in my arms like a sleepy child
far from its native land.

Above the clouds
dawn played its rosy finger exercises.

Life was being written on a clean white page.

And I read in our own language the psalms
that regulate the alliance of a Celtic lineage
on two shores
in church
in that spring of sleet in Ireland.

And there I read verse by verse:
        'Enter with all the honour of a princess
        into the winter palaces.
Do not forget your native land.'

The Harps of Iwerddon (2005)

31

Benvida a "San Felicísimo"

Estou na vosa casa de Bínn Eadair
chegan os nenos con ofrendas
e vós con flores e coidados sen lindes
no fascinio da hora

e Shiva lame as mans que agariman
e mírame cos ollos ambarinos
no misterio das formas animais que amabamos

e ti falabas por símbolos de patria
e escribías un libro de historias e fragmentos
do Nilo
entrabas en ti mesma
traspasabas o tempo nunha imaxe fluvial
da raíña Nefertiti
que ofrece unha mandrágora a Akenaton

e todo se copiaba na virtual textura
dunha páxina nova

Hai un mantel moi branco
na longa mesa nórdica a carón da ventá
Paxaros e paxaros perseveran
na chuvia e nas consignas elevadas dun ceo
azul e errático de inverno

E agora cambia todo por cortesía das nubes
e miro a luz alternativamente
o sol menesteroso ou as aves que emigran
cara a ese azul que fuxe como un laio

As arpas de Iwerddon (2005)

Welcome to 'San Felicísimo'

I am in your house in Bínn Eadair.
Here come the children with their offerings
and you are everywhere with flowers and care without limit,
such is the fascination of the hour.

And Shiva licks the hands that caress her
and looks at me with amber eyes
in the mysterious way of animals that we have always loved.

And you are talking about symbols of a native land.
You were writing a book of stories and fragments
about the Nile.
You were entering into yourself
and piercing time in the fluvial image
of Queen Nefertiti
who offers a mandrake to Akenaton.

Now everything is being copied in the virtual texture
of a clean page.

There is a very white tablecloth
on your long Nordic table beside the window.
Birds and more birds keep persevering
in the rain and the high counsel of the winter sky,
blue and erratic.

And now, courtesy of the clouds, everything changes
and I, looking at the light, see alternatively
the needy sun or the migrating birds,
glimpsing that last ray of pale blue that flees like a moan.

The Harps of Iwerddon (2005)

Bosque de rododendros

Conversa con Mónica

Nesta mañá tan fría de Dublín nun domingo
de marzo
vaiamos miña nai á montaña de Howth
a ese lugar sagrado...

Dende aqueles outeiros pódese contemplar
a fábula da vida...

¿Pensas acaso que é ilusorio o deseño
do mar de Brân
seducido de xestas de prata e sortilexio
nesta saga irlandesa que estamos a asumir?
as velas liberadas da extinción
os invernos exánimes
o sal da marusía

e mesmo as fontes fundadas na intemperie
de Iwerddon
en tempos consagrados polas rulas do norde

Si. Pode ser todo efémero
todo tan fráxil como a flor de neve
Igual cás aves da memoria
e a caléndula virxe que apenas se respira...

Vamos axiña miña nai subamos
por corredoiras de vizosa lama cara ó bosque
de ilesos rododendros na montaña de Howth
onde aquel dolmen milenario xa sabes...

Aló por baixo das olladas
mora o reino dos Sidhe na vibración da luz
e a materia da chuvia...

Forest of Rhododendrons

Conversation with Monica

'On this freezing cold Dublin morning
in March
Mother, let us go to the Hill of Howth
and that sacred place of magic.

From the top of these hills you can contemplate
long and lonely, the fable which is life...'

'Do you think the patterns of Bran's sea
are an illusion?
Are the sea patterns being seduced by the gilded broom bushes
and the sorcery of this Irish saga we have come to accept?
The candles forever alight,
the winters without life,
the tang of the rough sea-salt

and even the fountains founded in weather-beaten
Iwerddon
in those times that were consecrated by the turtledoves of the North?'

'Yes. It may all be ephemeral
and as fragile as Edelweiss.
Whether as the birds of our memory
or the virgin marigold which we can hardly breathe.'

'Mother, let us hurry, to climb
along corridors of fertile mud towards that forest
of untouched rhododendrons that cover the Hill of Howth
there, beside that age-old dolmen that you know so well.'

'There, beneath our glances
lies the kingdom of the Sidhe, alive in the vibration of light
and the very substance of the rain.'

Eles poden deixar no corazón dos homes
unha flor moi liviana moi liviana...
ben saben os poetas
pensa en Yeats.

As arpas de Iwerddon (2005)

'They can create in the hearts of men
a flower, light, oh-so-light
that poets know so well.
Think of Yeats.'

The Harps of Iwerddon (2005)

Páxina Atlántica

Para Xesús Alonso Montero

Vin a aldea arredada no seu propio segredo
Nin se perdeu o celme inxel do Beatus Ille
Pasei a contemplar tanta fidelidade

Vin burriños cargados de herba e de xestas vivas
alpendres que harmonizan cos aparellos rústicos
a humilde ferramenta trasnoitada
ou tal vez encetar o pan de cada día signándolle
unha cruz por riba cun coitelo

Vin a camelia gaélica en Bínn Eadair
A paixón dos triskeles baixo o rigor dos liques
e da chuvia insubmisa
Vin pallozas e torques
e os míticos tesouros daquel reino de Tara

A cerimonia erótica do arado

Vin revelarse as antas na afinidade da morte
Todo se pode ler nesta páxina atlántica
na sustancia unitaria do narcisismo celta
Na camelia gaélica do xardín de Bínn Eadair

As arpas de Iwerddon (2005)

Page of the Atlantic

For Xesús Alonso Montero

Yes, I saw the village cut off and lost in its own secret.
Not even the slight flavour of *The Holy Isle* was lost.
I continued to think upon such infinity of fidelity.

I saw little donkeys loaded down with grass and live broom bushes
and sheds as battered as rustic utensils
and humble tools, long gone out of fashion
or even the way each day's bread is started, by marking it
on top in the shape of a cross with a knife.

I saw the Gaelic camellia that grows on Bínn Eadair.
I saw the passion of triskels in spite of the toughness of lichens
                                        and the insubordinate rain
I saw round towers and torques
and the mythical treasures of the Kingdom of Tara.

The erotic ceremony of ploughing.

I saw the dolmens reveal their affinity with death.
Everything can be read on this page of the Atlantic
in the unitary essence of the deep self-obsession of the Celts
which flowers in the Gaelic camellia in a garden in Bínn Eadair.

The Harps of Iwerddon (2005)

Avalon Avalon

... e contemplar contemplo na alma toda
aquela illa ensoñada diamante fuxidío
nin sei cómo arribara a esta terra mistérica
que se oculta e reserva
e souben que era a Illa de Emain Ablach
que chaman Avalon ou País das mazairas
só tiña na memoria aquela estrofa
incisa asumida no tempo:
        "Quel pays merveilleux que ce pays
        les jeunes n'y vieillissent point..."
e souben que era a terra das mazairas celestes
dos deuses hiperbóreos os donos do saber
da asolagada Atlántida
da asolagada Atlántida
da asolagada Atlántida...

...aquí non hai delirios nin paixón nin designios
hai camelias conscientes flores que deciden o aroma
a fragancia precisa para cada misterio:
crisantemos de inverno ou vellorita dos druídas
perennifolio acivro inda hoxe sacrosanto
ou glicinias exóticas consagradas a Dana...
...e a ti ofrendo Nai de todos os deuses
no ritmo boreal dos Tuatha Dé Danann
o alfabeto celeste
o dominio dos astros...

En Avalon hai ramas de brancura incisiva
froitos de ouro purísimo e moi fráxiles
como de vento extremo distanciado e sen patria
non son manxares para dar sustento
son unha forma esencial da concordia absoluta
unha visión total da suprema harmonía...

Avalon Avalon

... ar amharc timpeall dom chím iomlán an anama
an t-oileán ann/as , iathghlas, faoi chruth diamaint
níl a fhios agam fiú conas ar thangas i dtír ar an dtalamh rúnda
a cheileann agus a nochtann é féin
conas go raibh a fhios agam go rabhas tagaithe go hEamhain Úllach
ris a ráitear Oileán na n-Úll Cumhra
ní raibh fanta im chuimhne ach leathrann de bhéarsa
seachfhocal leathtaobhach gur glacadh leis thar am
                    "Quel pays merveilleux que ce pays
                    les jeunes n'y vieillissent point..."
agus bhí a fhios agam gurb é seo tír na gcrann úll neamhaí
tír na ndéithe iarbhórach, sealbhóirí na gaoise
ó thír Atlantis a chuaigh faoi thoinn
ó thir Atlantis a chuaigh faoi thoinn
is faoi thoinn...

... san áit seo níl aon speabhraídí , ná paisiúin, ná pleananna
tá bláthanna coinsiasacha caiméilia ann a roghnaíonn a gcuid cumhrachta
chun gurb ionann gach cumhracht agus rúndiamhair ar leith: —
criosaintemuim geimhridh nó nóiníní na ndraoíthe
an cuileann síorghlas atá fós beannaithe
nó an visteáiria andúchasach atá tiomnaithe do Dana...
agus duitse a ofráilim, a Mhathair na ndéithe
rithim tuaisceartach na dTuatha Dé Danann
an aibítir neamhaí
sealúchas na réalt...

In Eamhain Úllach tá craobhacha de bháine chomh fíor
torthaí den ór is glaine , atá fíor-leochailleach
faoi mar a bheadh camfheothain gaoithe a chuaigh áit éigin ar strae
gan talamh dúchais ar bith
ní sóláistí iad seo ar son beatha
is foirm riachtanach iad den gcomhcheol bunúsach
pictiúr iomlán den sárchomhchórda ...

Oh música enigmática que vén de nin se sabe!
música que non se explica por salterios nin cítaras nin arpas!
Oh luz radiante! Oh música que escurece os sentidos!
Oh rosa sen mudanza que fire docemente!
Oh eternidade que acende vida e morte
nunha chama vivísima no exterminio da rosa...!

As arpas de Iwerddon (2005)

Ó, seoithín seó, a cheoil rúnda ná feadar éinne cad as a dtagann sé
ceol nach mínítear i dtéarmaí saltaire nó ziotair nó cláirsí
A sholais ghléinigh, a cheoil a bhodhrann na céadfaithe
A róis bhuain, a ghortaíonn ar chuma chomh séimh
A shíoraíocht, a loisceann beatha agus bás
sa lasair bheo is cúis díothaithe don rós.

Cláirseacha Iwerddon (2005)

MARÍA DO CARME KRUCKENBERG

and

ANNE LE MARQUAND HARTIGAN

Irish Translation by
RITA KELLY

Falemos das acusacións incorrectas...

Falemos das acusacións incorrectas
respecto aos resultados dexenerativos,
que levan a traxedia irreflexiva
a calquera parte insostíbel.

(Un can famélico, perdido polas rúas,
non sabe abaiar a tristura.
Anda perdido).

Ti e mais eu tamén andamos
perdidos, irremisiblemente.
Xa sabes, eu quería subir ata a montaña
estendendo o meu mirar
ata o alén da responsabilidade.
E xa ves, estou aquí soa. Ás veces falo...

(Aínda non atopei o can perdido.
Probablemente morreu de incomprensión).

As complexas mareas da noite (2006)

46

Let's Talk about False Accusations...

Let's talk about false accusations
corrupt results
that take mindless tragedy
to some unbearable place.

(A famished dog abandoned in the streets
doesn't know how to howl its misery.
It is lost).

Quite inexcusably you and I
are wandering lost.
You know, I wanted to climb up to the mountain
gazing right out over everything
beyond all responsibility.
And you see, I am here alone. Sometimes I speak...

(I have still not found the lost dog.
It probably died of despair).

The Complex Tides of the Night (2006)

Non sei como fun pisando...

Non sei como fun pisando
tanta pedra, tanto asfalto
tanta terra.

Non sei que foi de tanta
chuvia, de tanta neve,
de tanto inverno.

Non sei nada de tanta area,
de tanto mar,
de tanto Agosto.

Non sei que foi do meu cabalo,
do meu can,
de tanto espacio, de tanto brado.

Non sei do que foi,
"¡tanto de tanto!"
e agora a penas nada.
Un sopro de silencio
no medio desta calma.

As complexas mareas da noite (2006)

Ní Aithním mo Choischéim Fhéin...

Ní aithním mo choischéim fhéin
Ar an gcarraig, an méid sin asfailt
An domhan uile.

Níl fhios agam cá ndeachaigh an méid sin
báistí, an méid sin sneachta,
an geimhradh féin fiú.

Níl fhios agam tada faoin méid sin gainimh
Is na farraigí fairsinge,
Lúnasa féin ag cur thar maoil.

Cá bhfuil mo chapall, níl fhios agam,
Nó cá bhfuil mo mhadra-sa, cad tá tarlaithe
Cá ndeachaigh an méid sin spáis, is an tafann uile.

Níl fhios agam faic faoin am atá thart
An oiread is an iomarca le cois
Anois, is ar éigean rud ar bith
Ach séideán suimhnis
I gcroílár an chalm chiúnais seo.

Taoidí casta na hOíche (2006)

O cristal axústase...

O cristal axústase
a ese murmurio da rúa,
do ir e vir das multitudes
que percorren o deterioro
do comportamento alleo.
Maniféstase nas pintadas
que racionalizan a mentira
e traizoan
o patrimonio da intelixencia.
Andan dunha beira á outra
do territorio do adversario
e non matinan
nas consecuencias tolas
dos testemuños noxentos
que contribúen a ese proceder
do asasinato inmerecido
das almas transparentes.
A vida vai teledirixida;
vai arredor de fíos invisíbeis
xustificando o engano
coa palabra liberdade,
mentres os espíritos inocentes
choran e choran
polo erro insalvábel da caridade.

As complexas mareas da noite (2006)

The Mirror Reflects...

The mirror reflects
the murmur from the street,
the goings and comings of crowds
that hover around the disintegration
of other people's behaviour.
It shows itself in the graffiti
that gives substance to lies
and betrays
the possession of intelligence.
They shift from side to side
of the enemy's territory
and don't consider
the crazy consequences
of the sickening evidence
that adds to that behaviour
of the undeserved murder
of clear souls.
Life is remote-controlled;
it goes along invisible tracks
justifying lies
with the word freedom,
while innocent spirits
cry and cry
because of the insurmountable
failure of love.

The Complex Tides of the Night (2006)

Lembro aqueles tempos do verán...

Lembro aqueles tempos do verán
tomando o sol
e refrescando os corpos
no mar.
Recordo cando tocabas
os meus labres
cos dedos mollados
de auga e de sal.
Eramos tan nós mesmos
tan lonxe da realidade
tan inconscientes da barbarie
que non tiñamos horizonte
máis que na profundidade
da mirada
centrada nos ollos do encanto.
Ti e mais eu envoltos
na area da inocencia
gozando da liberdade
que roubamos
os desfarrapados da historia.

As agullas do reloxo
pasando mansamente
para achegar as tebras
da inxustiza.

Agora xa é tarde para todo,
case que é tarde para todo,
ata permanecer perdidos
neste espello.

Os límites do arreguizo (2008)

I Remember Those Summer Days...

I remember those summer days
sunbathing—
dipping our bodies
in the sea.
I remember you would touch
my lips
with your fingers wet
with water and salt.
We—so ourselves
so far from reality so
unaware of cruelty
our only horizon the depths
of delight in our gazing eyes.
You and I wrapped up
in the sands of innocence
revelling in our stolen freedom
history's tattered ones.

The hands of the clock
creep gently bringing
dark injustice closer.

Now—it's too late already,
it's almost too late for everything,
even for lingering lost
in this mirror.

Shiver's Limits (2008)

Recordas como ladraba...

A Dolores Fernández

Recordas como ladraba
un can
aquel amañecer?

Tiñamos unha preguiza
que non deixaba
poñer un pé
no entarimado frío
do mes de novembro.
Pola outra banda
aínda tiña teus labres
esvarando pola miña
caluga.
Fíxose imposíbel voltar
ó traballo e á rutina
diaria.
Non sei si recordas
aqueles tempos
de loita agachada
dos noso corpos
recén estreados...

Foi fermoso, foi moi fermoso
ter vivido.

Os límites do arreguizo (2008)

Do You Remember How the Dog...

For Dolores Fernández

Do you remember how the dog
barked
that dawn?

We—full of a languor
that forbade us
put a foot
on the cold floorboards
of November.
I still had your lips
slipping down my spine.
Impossible for me to return
to boring work—the daily
grind.
I don't know if you remember
those times
of the secret struggle
of our bodies
in their first touch...

It was beautiful,
it was very beautiful
to be alive.

Shiver's Limits (2008)

XOHANA TORRES

and

CELIA DE FRÉINE

Penélope

DECLARA o oráculo:
   "Que á banda do solpor é mar de mortos,
   incerta, última luz, non terás medo.

   Que ramos de loureiro erguen rapazas.
   Que cor malva se decide o acio.

   Que acades desas patrias a vindima.
   Que amaine o vento, beberás o viño.

   Que sereas sen voz a vela embaten.
   Que un sumario de xerfa polos cons".

Así falou Penélope:

   "Existe a maxia e pode ser de todos.
   ¿A que tanto nobelo e tanta historia?

   EU TAMÉN NAVEGAR".

Tempo de ría (1992)

Penelope

Dar leis an oracal:
"Go bhfuil muir na marbh lámh le himeall an fhordhorcha,
a léas deireanach, éideimhin, ná bíodh faitíos ort.

Go n-ardaíonn ainnireacha pósaetha labhrais.
Go gcruthaíonn crobhaingí fíonchaora a liathchorcra féin.

Go sábhála tú na fíonchaora ó chríocha na sinsear.
Go síothlaí an ghaoth, go n-óla tú an fíon.

Go réaba maighdeana mara gan ghlór an seol.
Go gcúra treise an chúir na sceireacha".

Mar seo a labhair Penelope:

"Is ann don draíocht, le cách í a shealbhú.
Tuige an t-íorna uile is an oiread leithscéal?

CROCHFAIDH MISE MO SHEOL FÉIN".

Am an Inbhir (1992)

59

Ofelia

O bóreas sempre sopra polo norte,
entre as follas escuras dos alerces
nas almeas onde a néboa se axita.

A doncela que canta como nena
ten unha palidez case de morta:
Ofelia, man de plumas, a guirlanda
de fiuncho, de xarxa e trinitarias.

Lamenta Dinamarca esa loucura,
desequilibrio que conmove a herba
e enmudece os cisnes dos estanques.

Boa Ofelia, o amor nunca se sabe.
Unhas veces, como vir Deus a nós,
roce a penas pola pel das cereixas,
coroación de bicos nas murallas.
Roto o espello cos cen rostros do outro,
qué difícil manter dentro do peito
as promesas que non levou o vento,
fume de incendios, restos da batalla.
Dese modo, o amor, case nos mata.
E ti, tan inocente, no seu nome,
perdes as horas a tecer metáforas.

Todas morremos no curso que é a vida,
nós mesmas, expoliadas na vixilia,
o sol que se demora nos marmelos,
entrar na sombra, vulnerar a noite.

Doente e soa, ao límite do ocaso,
terás un ceo duro, sen estrelas,
podes romper a luz como unha rama:
na escuridade brillarán teus ollos.
Perdida Ofelia, como un río de rosas.

Vigo, April 2000
Published in *O Correo Galego*, 5 October, 2000

Ophelia

The Boreas blows from the north
soughing through dark larch leaves
in the battlements where fog lurks.

The maiden who sings like a child
is almost as pale as death:
Ophelia, your under-wave hand,
garland of sage, pansy and rue.

Denmark mourns that madness—
the lost poise that stirs the grass,
makes mute those swans on the mere.

Good Ophelia, love is never realised.
At times, like when God appears,
it grazes the skin of cherries,
crowns those walls with kisses.
The mirror cracked by the other's myriad faces,
how hard to hold within our heart
promises not stolen by the wind,
smoke from fires, battle remains.
This is how love almost smites us.
And you, so innocent, weave
metaphors in its name.

We die many times during life,
robbed of being even while awake,
the sun lingers on the quince trees,
to enter shade, pierce the night.

Alone and infirm, a starless sky
will await you at the edge of dusk:
though your life snap like a branch,
your eyes will shine in the dark.
Lost Ophelia, like a burn of roses.

Vigo, April 2000
Published in *O Correo Galego*, 5 October, 2000

Sibila en Ribadavia

Protéxeme, crepúsculo,
lugar dos meus exvotos,
humilde acudo ao sol en rogativa.
Ás voltas coas andadas,
buscar na infancia
o tesouro do mapa oculto baixo as pedras.
En min sempre levita Lola ingrávida,
cun acompañamento sonoro de pardais,
seu perfil en realce pola extrema.
Sibila en Ribadavia, chambra moura,
bendita sexa a que esmagaba os acios
para facer o viño como se fose a luz,
¡canto amor aínda move!
Nesta hora, amparada a poñente,
Peregrino ata o mundo amatista das viñas:
é que nada se entenderá de todo
se antes non regreso ao punto de partida.
Non me permite a morte
alcanzar o recanto por onde Lola asoma
como un doce debuxo de Chagall.

Eu tamén navegar (entry speech for the Royal Galician Academy, 2001)

Sybil in Ribadavia

Twilight, my votive place,
protect me. Supplicant,
I face the sun at this vigil hour.
Adopting old habits once again,
searching in childhood for the map,
the treasure concealed beneath crags.
Lola, resonant with sparrow-song,
takes hold of me, as ever,
her shape in relief at the edge of our being.
Sybil in Ribadavia, black-garbed,
blessed be she who trampled grapes,
making light of wine,
still the source of so much love.
Now, sheltered from the westerly,
pilgrim who recalls the amethyst vineyards:
the essence of life will not be grasped
unless I return to the beginning.
Death keeps me from the verge
where Lola inclines
as though from a print by Chagall.

I Too Shall Navigate (entry speech for the Royal Galician Academy, 2001)

Chámome imaxe á malva luz da hora. Ás veces vén a néboa que me muda de todo

Corpo tendido pola area, rapaza melancólica.
Cando te ergues lixeira e moves os cabelos
eu me semello a ti, creación noutra praia.

Comunican as Illas ese filtro irreal
de luminarias no corazón celeste.

Eramos crédulos mais pasou o tempo.
(O soño está na luz que nos cega un instante)

De súpeto a paisaxe varía despiadada,
desaparece a moza de bañador vermello,
hai unha voz que a chama entre os millos.

Arestora o misterio fica no horizonte.
Todo ten a tristeza de sentirnos alleos
mentres polo serán Venus asoma.

Tempo de ría (1992)

64

My Name Is Image in the Hour's Mauve Light. At Times the Fog That Transforms Me Descends

Body lying on the sand, pensive lass.
Seeing you on that far beach, rise up easy
and shake your hair, reminds me of myself.

The Islands, lit by the evening sun,
manifest in an ethereal sequence.

We believed, blinded for an instant
by dream-light, but time passed.

Without warning, or regard, a scene change:
the lass in the red swimsuit vanishes,
summoned by a voice from within the maize.

The enigma lingers on the horizon.
Everything sad as though kept at bay
while the Evening Star appears.

Estuary Time (1992)

Sempre baixaba pola Praza Vella...

Sempre baixaba pola Praza Vella
onde nenos xogaban a moedas
no mercado dos peixes.
O recalmón callaba polas mesas
un bafo insoportable, das agallas
que arrincaban de cedo as vendedoras.

Ao lonxe, o mar máis bo,
as hélices grisallas do Estaleiro,
portalóns do Arsenal, altos, escuros,
gastados pola chuvia.
As aves sempre
coma unha independente caravana
desvirtuando o voo...
ah, don tremendo de bater ao aire.

Infancia, pasos meus, irrevocable sombra
é todo o que me queda da túa noite.

Pradeirío do Tempo, campo ileso,
gozar de maio para as miñas pombas:
¡como delega a vida esa dozura
que abrigaba na porta co teu nome!

Sen matinar aínda que eternos non serían
cantares de altas gorxas
a quencernos un pouco coma apertas pequenas.

Sen saber nada aínda das dúas bandas
que dividen, perdidamente, aos homes,
se dous algunha vez se recoñecen.

Many's the Time I'd Wend My Way through the Old Square...

Many's the time I'd wend my way through the Old Square
where children played push-penny
in the fish market.
The tables heavy
with the stench from gills,
earlier ripped out by fishwives.

Far off the calm sea,
grisaille shipyard hulks,
tall martial gangways
corroded by rain.
As always the birds
in formation, swooping,
a law unto themselves,
their unique gift for beating the air.

Childhood, my prints, an immutable shade
is all that remains of your night.

Meadow of time, untilled pasture
beloved of doves in May:
how life delegates the dulcet
that I shielded within your portal.

While not yet knowing
the high-pitched hymns that held us
in warm embrace would be of little solace.

While not yet comprehending the two sides
that set men apart
once they have recognised each other.

Pois conxúranos un ebrio testamento de anos,
un esqueleto ao mar, que non devolve
nin tan sequera florecido un óso.

¿Non o sabiades?
Nada é ese acougo transitorio, de beira:
O mar perto da area, que xa é mesmo
que dicir a Morte.

Estacións ao mar (1980)

For we have drunk the years, bewitched,
as a skeleton to the sea
that returns not a single bone.

Hadn't you realised?
The passing calm of the seaside counts for naught:
the sea borders the sand
and that is as good as saying Death.

Seasons to the Sea (1980)

MARILAR ALEIXANDRE

and

MARY O'MALLEY

Irish Translation by
MARTIN NUGENT

derrotas domésticas

debeu ser moi difícil
degolar as anguías
sen cortar os dedos
arrandearte para que non te cubrisen
as escamas do ollomol
liscar do nó corredío das sabas

nas noites opacas
que batallas contra os garavanzos
medrando disformes na agua   que absurda tarefa
escoller lentellas de arroz
que impotencia
cando o leite fervido vai por fóra
inevitablemente

e se o batifundo das tixolas
non che deixaba oír a música
se o teu francés e alemán
eran inútiles contra a graxa nos fogóns
se os tubos de agua berran como nenos
ou gaivotas e   as patacas se pegan
no fondo da tarteira

nai
¿como é que estás sorrindo nas fotos?

Catálogo de velenos (1999)

domestic defeats

it must have been very hard
beheading eels
without cutting your fingers
twisting to avoid the scales of sea bream
escaping through the slip knot of the bed sheets

such wars you fought
in the dim nights
against the chickpeas growing   monstrous in the water
and picking lentils from grains of rice
what a ridiculous task!
such helplessness
when the boiled milk overflows
unstoppable

and if the din of the frying pans
stopped you hearing music
if your French and German
were in vain against the grease on the stove
and the pipes sounded like babies
or seagulls and   the potatoes stuck
to the bottom of the pot

why are you smiling in the photographs
mother?

Catalogue of Poisons (1999)

o diario (3 rabuda)

e teño bastante mal xenio

(aquí acaba o diario)
acertaches   poñendo o punto
despois da contundente descrición

é rabuda coma min
puideches escribir
non acepta sen protestar
que o luns siga ó domingo
nin negociaría   como Brancaneves
un acougo ó prezo de cociñar   lavar
coser e calcetar

é impaciente de máis
usa as palabras para cortar
tesoiras mal afiadas
do espello copia o meu desdén
non ten boa relación coas esquinas
dos mobles   que lle meten cambadelas
e deixan marcas negras dos seus beliscos.

herdou de min os ósos pequenos
a má uva   a lingua gallada
a tinta ou veleno que lle brota baixo as uñas
vén de moi atrás
e aínda que se negue a recoñecelo
fun eu quen lle aprendeu
a enfiar palabras

Catálogo de velenos (1999)

74

the diary (3 surly)

and I have a temper on me

(the diary ends here)
you were right   to put a full stop
after such a blunt description

she is surly like me
you could have written
that she wouldn't agree
that Monday follows Sunday
she would never make Snow White's bargain—
washing and cooking
and knitting and sewing
in exchange for shelter

she is too impatient
she uses words to cut—
like badly sharpened scissors
it is my disdain that she copies from the mirror
and she is awkward around furniture
the corners   trip her up
and mark her with blue black bruises

she has inherited my small bones
my moods   my forked tongue
the ink or poison that flows from her fingernails
comes from way back
and even if she won't admit it
it was I who taught her
how to string words

Catalogue of Poisons (1999)

varrer as cinzas

no lar morrerá o lume
prendido hai catro séculos
e non vou recoller o tizón
caído da túa man
                    pai

á noite varrerei as cinzas
aínda que escorrente as ánimas
dos antepasados,
esgazando deles
callóns de lembranzas

se a cheminea
cala as súas palabras de fume
gritando en silencio
a soidade da casa
non me tomes a requesta
¿por que a min de cinco irmáns?

os rachóns no unllar
agromarán novas raíces
volverán termar da terra
sen ninguén que os queime.

na cociña que o lume non quece
aínda bate o eco da túa voz
lendo libro tras libro   plantando
en nós
semente de vento

Desmentindo a primavera (2003)

76

sweeping up the ashes

Father

the fire lit in the hearth
four centuries ago will die out
and I will not pick up the half burned log
that has fallen from your hand

I will sweep away the ashes at night
even if it drives away the ancestors
their souls bleeding clots of memory
as they flee.

if the chimney swallows its words of smoke
screaming in the silence
of the lonely house do not reproach me,
why me out of five brothers?

the firewood in the shed
will grow new roots
they will clutch the earth again
without a soul to burn them

in the kitchen the fire fails to warm
the echoes of your voice still beat
reading book after book   sowing
us with the seeds of the wind

Denying Spring (2003)

luis

nacín no día de Bealtain
logo da noite de Walpurgis
e aínda que ninguén pendurou
no meu berce
unha póla de capudre
atada con fío vermello
nin creo nos celtas
o capudre escolleume para esgazar a súa vara
sen coitelos
cantar os seus froitos encarnados
inscritos coa estrela de cinco puntas
como ourizos de mar

nacín no día de maio
que lembra Haymarket
o vermello protexíanos desde a bandeira
agochada entre as enaguas
precisabamos levar naquela barca
algo máis que varas de capudre
para conxurar as tormentas

é mágoa
renegar dos usos tradicionais
chantar espeques de capudre nas tumbas
para que os mortos non se incorporen
á roldiña
anoar gromos aos rabos das vacas
amorear rachas de capudre nas fogueiras
para queimar as bruxas

Abecedario de árbores (2006)

luis

Lá Bealtaine a rugadh mé
i ndiaidh oíche Walpurgis
is fiú murar chroch éinne géag chaorthainn
snaidhmthe le snáithe dearg
os cionn mo chliabháin
is fiú mura gcreidim sna Ceiltigh
roghnaigh an caorthann mise
chun a ghéag a bhaint
gan usáid sceana
chun a chaora dearga a bhlaiseadh
inscríofa mar chrosóg mhara
lena réaltaí cúig rinn

Lá Bealtaine a rugadh mé
tráth chomórtha mhargadh an fhéir
chosain an deirge muid ón mbratach
faoi cheilt inár bhfo-sciortaí
bhí gá le níos mó ná maidí caorthainn
sa bhárc úd
lenár gcoscaint ó anfaí

is trua
na sean-nósanna a shéanadh
ag ropadh cuaillí caorthainn in uaigheanna
chun na mairbh a chosc
dul ar oilithreacht na n-anamnacha
ag ceangal bachlóga ar eireabaill bó
ag carnadh géaga caorthainn
ar thinte cnámh
chun cailleacha feasa a loscadh

Aibítir na gCrann (2006)

79

comedores de cabezas

despreguei aos ventos todas as miñas velas
Metamorfoses, XV, 176-177

ao comer cabezas de peixe
recoñecémonos entre nosoutros
por fillos das náiades
nas veas levamos salitre
—usámolo ás veces para fabricar pólvora—
e dos vultos a carón das orellas
nos días de temporal
nada digas: son garlas

ao comungar coas cabezas do peixe
reclamamos a herdanza das espiñas
facémolas nosas gorxa abaixo
vea arriba
atravesando no seu eixe sutil
palabras dun poema

houbo un tempo en que comiamos peixe cru
e respirabamos na auga
compartiamos simetría pentámera
            con ourizos e estrelas
nadabamos máis veloces que as luras

agora, para cruzar as augas,
debemos confiarnos
ao Nordés nas velas

Mudanzas (2007)

the head eaters

To the winds I unfurled all my sails

Metamorphoses, XV, 176-177

when we eat fish heads
we know
we are children of the naiads
who carry saltpeter in our veins
—sometimes we use it to make gunpowder—
the less said the better
about those swellings above our ears
on stormy days
they are gills

when receiving our communion of fish heads
we claim our heritage of fish-bones
we reclaim them in the throat
in the veins
as they send the words of poems
circling along their cunning trajectories

there was a time when we ate raw fish
we breathed underwater
we shared five-armed symmetry
        with sea urchins and starfish
we swam faster than squid

in order to cross the seas these days
we have to trust ourselves
to the North eastern wind in our sails

Shiftings (2007)

LUZ PICHEL

and

CATHERINE PHIL MacCARTHY

Poema prólogo

Hai nesta aldea un gato
que coñece os abismos.

Ás noites,
desde o Alto das Penas,
érguese e mira para a casa que fora do seu dono
e laia coma un cadelo adoecido.
A súa sombra é longa e afiada.
Espétaselle a un no peito de por vida.

Vai haber que o matar.

Casa pechada (2006)

Prologue Poem

This village has a cat
that knows the depths.

At night,
from the Summit of Sorrow,
he rises up and peers at the house
that belonged to his master
and wails like a stricken dog.
His shadow is long and keen.
It pierces one's breast for life.

He has to be put down.

Locked House (2006)

Queimar a leña

A néboa do amañecer énchese de trafego
de xente voandeira.
O canto dun galo que vén de lonxe
correspóndese co canto do corvo
que foxe escorrentado
polos golpes dos homes.

Érguense co día e rompen mazas
contra as portas do gando.

Outro galo respóndelle.
Miro para o cuberto da leña e penso
como me gustaría dala queimado toda.

Casa pechada (2006)

Burning the Firewood

The fog at daybreak is crammed with the bustle
of rushing people.
A cock's cry that comes from afar
echoes the cry of the crow,
that scurries frightened
by the blows of men.

They rise with the day and break maces
against the doors of the cattle shed.

Another cock responds.
I look at the woodshed and think
how I would like to burn it all.

Locked House (2006)

Pésanlle as pólas á figueira coa carga dos figos

Á mañá cedo, pésanlle á figueira nas follas
as bonecas da néboa
e dá uns paseíños polo prado
coma unha muller preñada.

Andan aos figos os bonecos do aire
e fan a súa festa
tocan as castañolas
asubían
fan soar as tesoiras do afiador
rinse do mundo.

E a figueira,
aliviada e contenta
move as follas e mira para min,
que me quedo sen figos,
boneco a carón do espantallo que caeu para o chan:

Descansa á miña sombra,
escaravella na terra un pouco
a ver se encontraras unha pataquiña:
Pésanche moito os fardos.
Ti non es un animal do aire.

Casa pechada (2006)

The Branches of the Fig Tree Are Laden with Its Crop of Figs

In the early morning, the fig tree's leaves are laden
with dolls of the mist,
and it walks around the meadow
like a pregnant woman.

The action men of the air are after the figs
and they have their feast,
play the castanets,
they whistle,
roar at the blades of the knife grinder,
laugh at the world.

And the fig tree
relieved and content,
stirs her leaves and looks at me
who is left without figs,
doll at the foot of the scarecrow fallen to the ground:

Rest in my shadow,
scatter the earth a little,
seek to find a tasty potato:
Your bundles weigh deeply.
You are not a creature of the air.

Locked House (2006)

Non se sabe case nada

Pinga o orballo da folla do feixón
mentres os gatos brincan e foxen
da herba mollada.

Dous paxaros moi grandes pasan
voando na néboa
ao ras das coles do galiñeiro.
Que quererán?

E esa muller que berra no Souto coma unha tola,
por quen chamará tan cedo?
quen lle escapou esta noite coa filla?

Ladran os cans,
estou soa na casa?

Casa pechada (2006)

Almost Nothing Is Known

The dew drips from the leaf of the bean plant
while the cats play and slip away
from the wet grass.

Two very large birds pass by
flying in the mist
level with cabbages of the henhouse
What are they after?

And that woman who screams from the heights like a mad one,
for whom might she be calling so early?
Who ran off this night with her daughter?

The dogs bark,
am I alone at home?

Locked House (2006)

Sachando na horta

Esa muller leva toda a vida plantando as mesmas coles,
cravando na terra os mesmos chuzos,
deitándose cos homes ao pé do regueiro, parindo soa
ao pé dun regueiro.
Ás noites ouvea polos camiños e ninguén a escoita.
Agora ten unha filla que aprendeu a ler.

Casa pechada (2006)

Ag Grafadh san Úllord

Chaith an bhean sin a saol iomlán ag cur na cabáistí céanna,
Ag sá na maidí céanna sa chré,
Ina luí le fir cois an tsrutháin,
Ag saolú linbh ina haonar cois an tsrutháin.
San oiche bíonn sí amuigh ag caoineadh ar fud na cosáinn
ach aird ar bith ní thugann éinne di.
Anois ta iníon aici, gur feidir léithi léamh.

Teach Faoi Ghlas (2006)

CHUS PATO

and

LORNA SHAUGHNESSY

Irish Translation by
RITA KELLY

PORQUE NON É SÓ O IDIOMA O QUE ESTÁ AMEAZADO...

PORQUE NON É SÓ O IDIOMA O QUE ESTÁ AMEAZADO
SENÓN A NOSA PROPIA CAPACIDADE LINGÜÍSTICA, sexa cal sexa
o idioma que falemos

A LINGUA É PRODUCCIÓN, a lingua produce, produce COMUNICACIÓN
PRODUCE PENSAMENTO, PRODUCE CAPACIDADE POÉTICA,
produce ganancia e beneficio, PRODÚCENOS como HUMANOS,
prodúcenos como FELICIDADE

A lingua é PRODUCCIÓN, de aí os intentos do CAPITAL por PRIVATIZAR
a lingua, por deixarnos SEN PALABRAS

A LINGUA, calquera LINGUA NO CAPITAL, tende ao esvaecemento,
tende a converterse en algo que se consume. En algo que xa non
PRODUCIMOS os falantes, senón que o CAPITAL, no seu intento de
privatizarnos, PRODUCE PARA NÓS

No CAPITAL os/as creadoras da Lingua, @s falantes, pasan a ser

CONSUMIDORES; a Lingua, calquera Lingua no Capital, pasa a ser un
producto de consumo, o mesmo que calquera outra MERCADORÍA

LINGUA-SERVIDUME LINGÜÍSTICA
KAPITAL-KILLER
ASASINA

m-Talá (2000)

BECAUSE IT IS NOT ONLY LANGUAGE THAT IS THREATENED...

BECAUSE IT IS NOT ONLY LANGUAGE THAT IS THREATENED
BUT OUR VERY ABILITY TO SPEAK, in whatever
tongue that may be

LANGUAGE IS PRODUCTION, language produces, produces
COMMUNICATION, PRODUCES THOUGHT, PRODUCES THE
ABILITY TO WRITE, produces wealth and benefit, PRODUCES US as
HUMANS, produces us as JOY

Language is PRODUCTION, which is why CAPITAL attempts to PRIVATISE
language, to leave us WITHOUT WORDS

LANGUAGE, any LANGUAGE WITHIN CAPITALISM, tends to evaporate,
tends to change into something consumable. Something we no longer
PRODUCE as speakers, but that CAPITAL, in its attempt to privatise us,
PRODUCES FOR US

Within CAPITALISM, the creators of Language, the wo/men who speak it,
become

CONSUMERS, and Language, any Language within Capitalism, becomes a
consumer product, like any other MERCHANDISE

LANGUAGE-LINGUISTIC SERVITUDE
KAPITAL-KILLER
KILLS

m-Talá (2000)

A voz era pánico...

A voz era pánico
e desexaba, insistía, ter hábito(s) no poema

....

pero non todo pode ser transportado (non a voz, desde logo)

si *o espírito que invade ao bardo, entre as uces irtas*

e porque chove, os habitantes do poema teñen que abrir os seus
paraugas // sacan o que levan dentro e búscanlle acomodo fóra

[só porque ti pousas a mirada no texto podo comezar coas solucións]

isto é o que consegue Cabaleiro Amábel, facer que seres
alienados se presenten ante o mundo, e moi ao seu pesar, como
persoas ceibes

pero só a voz empasta as tres historias
a voz que a escritura non acubilla

así pois, un poeta é un ser ancián.

Máis que entrar o mundo dentro do poema
botar por fóra a escritura, como unha lava lene e transparente,
muselina

tanto ceo
tanta primavera

ves, isto é un acto político: torcerlles a vontade aos que
obedecen

pero falta o contexto.

The Voice Was Pure Panic...

The voice was pure panic
and desired, insisted on inhabiting the poem

....

but not everything can be transported (certainly not the voice)

not like *the spirit that possesses the bard in the midst of rugged heathers*

and because it's raining, the inhabitants of the poem have to
open their umbrellas / / take out all they have on the inside and
find place for it on the outside

[it is only because you lay your eyes on the text that I can begin
to find solutions]

this much Sincere Gent can do, make the marginalised visible to
the world, in spite of themselves, as free individuals

but only the voice can bind all three stories
the voice that writing fails to shelter

and so, a poet is an ancient being.

Rather than bring the world into the poem
pour out the written word. Like a transparent, light lava, muslin

so much sky
so much spring

you see, this is a political act: to twist the will of those who obey

but out of context.

E que dicir dos soportes!, cando xa o papel non atura e só é concibíbel unha parede e a proxección de letras dixitais (seguramente nun museo ou nos paneis da autoestrada) ou esas mesmas frases envolvendo como cintas luminosas os corpos dos viandantes que dialogan sobre o voar das aves ou os bucles dos miñatos que se mimetizan coas árbores cando estenden as ás coma un niño

a teoría é esa violencia ética do intanxíbel

e está o problema do eu, cantos? e das situacións

prefiro o meu pánico a entrar nas librerías, excluíndote a ti, que me abandonas en calquera lugar, sen cartos, ou dentro do coche sen freo de man. Visitamos unha cidade para lembrar os edificios das cidades

os soños non son teoría, e agora temos que quedar aquí porque ti non queres espertar, neste palacete de urbanización privada, con outros moitos e moitas da nosa condición. Esta noite os nosos asasinos están bébedos ou pechados no váter

dunha vez para sempre nada hermético, nin críptico (que nunca nosoutros escribimos) e pono xa en órbita, con todos os nosos espléndidos matos e carqueixas.

E fíxate como se torna doce a verdade, cando descalza te mantés, ingrávida?, na placenta dos amieiros

★★

as sinapses volven, a inquietante floración de abril

Hordas de escritura (2008)

And what about the medium? When the paper cannot take any more, all that's left is a wall and the projection of digital letters (no doubt in a museum or on the billboards alongside motorways) or amongst those very utterances that wind like bright ribbons around the bodies of passersby who discuss the nature of birds in flight or the loop of the kites that blend with the trees when they open out their wings like a nest

theory is that ethical violence of the intangible

and then there is the problem of the I, (how many?) and of circumstances

I prefer to panic going into bookshops, exclude you, you who abandon me in any old place, without a bean, or even in a car with no hand-break. We visit one city to remember the buildings of the others

dreams are not theory, and now we have to stay here because you don't want to wake, in this private development mansion, surrounded by wo/men in the same predicament. Tonight our murderers are drunk or locked in the toilet

for once and for all nothing hermetic, nothing cryptic (which we never write) and send it straight into orbit, with all our splendid gorse and broom

And look how the truth sweetens when you go barefoot and... weightless? In the placenta of the alders

★★

the synapses return, the disquiet of April in bloom

Hordes of Writing (2008)

Un cabalo para as musas

Fotografaron a morte, o ollo fascinado da morte: o espello, a pedra, os cabalos. Pero eu non creo que iso lle sucedese á morte; sen embargo a nai expulsa de si en cada pinga de sangue cabalos máis luminosos que a luz que son cabalos fonte, cabalos pozo, cabalos lóstrego e trono, que é o cabalo das musas.

O cabalo das musas é un nacente de auga, cando ves o lóstrego no ceo el xa non está, vai co son do trono cara o teu ouvido, cando se aquieta é pozo de auga profunda e podes reflectirte nel; se de inmediato recoñeces a túa imaxe quedas presa, se non a recoñeces nunca non poderás vivir, se a imaxe das augas é a do amado é que son entrañas.

A nai é alíxera e ás veces achégase cun cabalo, coida del e móntao, ela tamén pode transformarse en egua, a súa lingua é longa e babea como os cabalos. Cando a nai bota a lingua por fóra, a súa boca é reunión dos sexos. O cabalo das musas é o nacente de todos os ríos e coas augas viaxa polo planeta e vai dar ao mar, pero a súa linfa é doce, por iso non podemos dicir que as salinas malia a brancura e a brillantez pertenzan á nai. Durante meses o cabalo, as musas erguéronse antes de raiar a alba, querían escribir renunciando ás próteses da civilización, non co corpo senón con aquelas zonas do corpo retiradas a áreas de luxo e confort.

A nada está sempre presente nas palabras por iso as palabras son fantasmagorías da voz. Por esta causa as meniñas e os meniños adoran as tronadas.

Cando o sangue cobre o espello é a nai, é veraz e os paxaros son vermellos. Se a nai elixe o teu ollo para petrificar aos que te odian é porque sen dúbida e sen rival é o máis fermoso. A pedra conmemora o horror (cómpre que flúa que entre e saia do corpo o espanto) se é persoal, as estatuas son íntimas. O sangue empapa o mercurio, os riscos son entón incalculábeis e a víbora busca a vea.

Ningunha identificación é perfecta. Dis "madre /memoria".

Capall do na mBéithe

Thógadar grianghraf an bháis, súil mhealltach an bháis, an scáthán, an chloch, na capaill.

Ach ní ghlacaim leis gur tharla a leithéid i gcás an bháis, cibé ar bith, cuireann an mháthair uaithi i gcuile bhraon fola, capaill atá níos gile ná an solas féin, capaill foinse, capaill tobair, capaill tintrí is tóirní, sin é capall na mBéithe.

Is ionann capall na mBéithe is foinse uisce, nuair a fheiceann tú an tintreach sa spéir níl sé ann a thuilleadh, téann sé i dtreo do chluasa le torann tóirní, nuair a ligeann an stoirm fuithi is tobar doimhin é, d'fhéadfá thú fhéin a fheiceáil ann, má aithníonn thú d'íomhá féin láithreach déanfar príosúnach díot, muna n-aithnaíonn thú é ní fhéadfá bheith beo, más íomhá na páirte atá san uisce 'sé an fáth ná gur putóga iad.

Is coséadrom an mháthair, uaireanta tagann sí i láthair le capall, tugann sí aire dó, téann sí ar mharcaíocht air, d'fhéadfadh sí bheith ina lair, teanga fhada ag sileadh léi, seileann sí díreach cosúil le capall. Nuair a ghobann sí a teanga amach is ionann a béal is na h-inscní ag teacht le chéile. Is ionann capall na mBéithe is foinse gach abhann, is téann sé leis na h-uiscí, mórthimpeall an domhain is tagann sé chomh fada leis an bhfarraige, ach is uisce abhann atá aige, mar sin ní féidir linn a rá go mbaineann na riasc salainn, d'ainneoin a ghile is a bhántacht, leis an mháthair.

Le míonna anuas d'éirigh an capall is na Béithe sul má bhí an ghriain ann fiú, bhíodar ag iarraidh scríobh i gcoinne phrothésiseachaí na sibhialtachta, gan a bheith i gceist ach corp-pháirteanna seachas an corp fhéin, is iad imithe chuig limistéar bláfar is sólásach.

Tá an neamhní i láthair an fhocail i gcónaí, mar sin níl i bhfocal ach fantasmagória an ghlóir. Sin é an fáth go bhfuil buachaillí is cailíní chomh tugtha sin do phlimpeanna tóirní.
Nuair a chlúdaíonn an fhuil an scáthán, is é an mháthair é, 'sé an fhírinne é agus is dearg ar fad na héanlaithe.
Má roghnaíonn an mháthair do shúil chun cloch a dhéanamh astu a chothaíonn fuath dhuit, déanann sí é toisc nach bhfuil súil ar bith níos áille. Déanann an chloch cuimhneachán ar an uafás

Ela non te ve porque a ti agáchate a noite, se cadra un presentimento pola sombra ou cando se che reflicte o corpo na burga. Precisas un transporte veloz para chegar, para volver ao aire dos humanos. A cabeza que levas no fardel é máscara do teu rostro defunto. Non é persuasiva a morte, iletrada flor, bailarina do Hades. Tamén ti danzas ao son da frauta, do asubío das serpes, dos latexos dos cans, do rincho dos cabalos.

(unpublished)

(is mithid go ritheann an t-eagla trín chorp) más pearsanta é,
agus is dlúth ar fad na dealbha. Súnn an fhuil an t-airgead beo,
téann na fiontair thar maoil, téann an nathair i dtreo na féithe.
—Níl aitheantas ar bith fíor iomlán críochnaithe.
Déarann tú "máthair nó cuimhne".

Ní fheiceann sí thú toisc go bhfuil tú clúdaithe leis an oíche,
b'fhéidir réamheolas le scáth nó nuair a fhrithchaitheann do
cholainn i n-uisce te na foinse. Síob gasta de dhith ort, chun
teacht i dtír arís i n-aer an duine dhaonna. An cloigeann atá
agat sa mhála is aghaidh fidil e dod'aghaidh mhairbh fhéin. Níl
an Bás mealltach, bláth neamhliteartha, rinceoir ó Háidéas.
Déanann tusa rince chomh maith i nglór na feadóige móire, i
siosarnach nathrach, i dtafann madraí agus i seitreach na gcapall.

(Gan foilsiú)
Translated by Lorna Shaughnessy with Rita Kelly

ANA ROMANÍ

and

MAURICE HARMON

Os largartos vírona pasar...

Os lagartos vírona pasar
observaron o seu lento caer ensimesmado

Que estrañas formas perfila a dor
nos corpos exhaustos

Love me tender. 24 pezas mínimas para unha caixa de música (2005)

The Lizards Watched Her As She Passed...

The lizards watched her as she passed
and noted her gradual self-absorbed descent

What strange shapes pain inscribes
on wasted flesh

Love Me Tender. 24 Minimal Pieces for a Music Box (2005)

Por que sei que te vas ás veces...

Por que sei que te vas ás veces
e sinto o roce do teu corpo
contra as silveiras
Non esquezo.
Sei
Do longo camiño que te leva
do amor ó abandono
Presinto entón
tanta valentía
que andaría tebras e agonías
por ser a póla da memoria
que docemente te roza
cando volves
do silencio á miña roupa.

Das últimas mareas (1994)

110

Because I know You Sometimes Leave...

Because I know you sometimes leave
and feel your body tangle
with the thorns
I do not forget.
I know
how hard it is for you to move
from love to indifference.
At that moment I am so aware of
the grit it takes
I would descend through darkness and pain
to be the limb from the past
that softly trembles against you
when you turn
from silence to be part of me.

On the Last Tides (1994)

Fuga

En fuga as horas silvestres   estes corpos   a súa razón
aquelas amadas que andaron descalzas á beira do mundo
esa morna conquista da lei que anaina e regula
a greta   o cáliz   o seu acre sabor a fogar
En fuga o meu corpo nas tripas da historia e os seus relatos
ese amor que o fundou ecoico e romántico   a rosa   a súa espiña
a sombra delatada no rastro da usura e o capital
—tantas palabras que o uso nos rouba—En fuga
como abellas exhaustas ao caer da tarde   desprendidas do po
pole ou danza que algo reclama   Esta extenuación
Andaba coas puntas do pé   delicada non digo
senón crebada agarrada ao pánico
esta deformación que se impón a seres estraños
que perden o río   a rima   o rito   o ricto
tímidas e extremadamente útiles de teceláns   En fuga
quen construía a casa   as súas trampas   as hedras
sen sonetos   os vermes no suco dos cotenos   ese esforzo
que murmura debaixo dos cobertores   cristal fráxil cristal
Chantado na costa do século ven di o teu novo nome
a deflagración que o incendia   o caos no que se ordena
a paixón que o engastou   sublimes plebeas dispostas ao tango
extraviadas en fuga coa dor da costela e este cansazo
pois tanto Estado traga   regula a miña furia sen esplendor
agárrame as entrañas amor que desinstalo os teus dominios
así vaciada contemplo as túas gravuras as manchas que as auxilian
qué proclaman di   qué protexen di   de qué se apiadan
como gardan os lindes dos seus hortos a consigna
que repites   que atravesa   que instaura
cancións de mutiladas enfermas e cautivas que tanto Estado absorbe
qué nos ata di nesta mudanza quen nos ata que vixía
a creba desas artes   as danzas insurrectas
as pezas liberadas na mecánica da fuga
esta condición de tránsito grávida e magmática que a xerou

Love me tender. 24 pezas mínimas para unha caixa de música (2005)

Escape

The wild hours escape   these bodies   their reason
loves walked on bare feet at the edge of the world
mild subjection of the law that cradles and controls
the crack   the chalice   its bitter taste of home
My body escapes in the bowels of history and its yarns
love mimetic and romantic that founded it   the rose   its thorns
shadow glimpsed in the crush of usury and commerce
—many words custom takes from   us—Escaping
like tired bees when the day ends   freed of the dust
pollen or dance affirms something   This weariness
walking on the tips of its toes   I do not mean delicately
but crippled by an onslaught of panic
disfigurement imposed on strangers
who lose the river   the rhyme   the rite   the *rictus*
like the weaver-birds shy and purposeful   Escaping
the one building the home   its traps   its ivy
without sonnets   worms in the knuckle bones   that effort
murmurs beneath the blankets   oh so fragile   crystal
Nailed to the mast of the century you must declare your new name
upheaval that burns   chaos on which it rests
passion at its core   divine masses prepared to dance
lost in the escape with a stitch at the rib and this weariness
the State devours so much   controls my pathetic rage
love seize my bowels while I free myself from your supremacy
detached I look upon your etchings on stains colouring them
what do they affirm   what do they shelter   what do they pity
how are the borders of their orchards protected by the prohibition
that you repeat   that crosses   that secures
songs of patients wounded captives the State harbours
I would like to know what binds us in this action who binds us who guards
intricacies of those arts   rebellious dances
pieces loosed through the mechanism of escape
the transient condition gravid and magmatic that nurtured it

Love Me Tender. 24 Minimal Pieces for a Music Box (2005)

Que os cachalotes me suban polas pernas...

Que os cachalotes me suban polas pernas
e me deixen un rastro feroz de travesías

Que a súa pel me fale dos eclipses

que sexan eses corpos os rastros que debulle
cada tarde nas crebas
Que amen este perfil de raiba que desxea

Que me marquen
que as súas aletas aventen estímulos no empeño:
seguir

vivir ciclóns por dentro

Que saiban ser para o periplo
duras figuras de mar

amantes fríos que me queiman

Que eles mesmos rebenten en sal cando os reclame
que sexan nada cando nada sexa o que os nomea
abatida por golpes de luz
cando derrubo a casa ata os cimentos

Que me mollen a fronte no delirio
mentres percorro o arquipélago desorientado

as linguas perdidas das escravas que fun

Arden (1998)

Would That the Sperm Whales Would Climb My Legs...

Would that the sperm whales would climb my legs
and leave a tang of ocean wanderings

their skin speak to me of signs and wonders

may their bodies be the ways I shake loose
in each ravaging afternoon
I want them to love this spectre of yielding rage

I want them to stain me
their fins grow urgent in the approach:
not to stop

stirring up the interior with storms

They must know how to be along the way
merciless marine creatures

freezing lovers who burn me

May they themselves explode in salt when I hold them
may they be nothing when there is nothing that defines them
struck dumb by bolts of illumination
when I pull the house down to its joists and underpinnings

May they salve my temples when I go astray
traverse headlands of incomprehension

I   the displaced tongues of the dispossessed

Blazing (1998)

No medio da praza...

No medio da praza
despezan os restos da balea

Un corte limpo
e aquí temos os pulmóns
e aquí a cría que nunca fecundou o espólio
e aquí   superficial   a vaíña do pánico
que confundiu a monstra
por millas de océano   Órganos olfativos
en regresión e unha vista débil
que arrastrou a mole por labirínticas
intuicións do espanto

A balea non ten aletas!   Mírase unha nena

¿Por onde navegou mamífera a arqueoloxía da sombra?
A rapaza sorrí:

"Por min mesma   señores   por min mesma"

Arden (1998)

Lár na Cearnóige...

I lár na cearnóige
Réabann siad iarsmaí an mhíl mhóir ina bpíosaí

Glanbhuille amháin
is nochaítear na scámhóga
is an cruth a raideadh go fíochmhar
agus anseo—ar dhromchla—truaill an scaoill
a sheol an ollphéist ar seachrán
thar leithead ábhalmhór na bóchna
Teip ar chumas boltanach
agus radharc imithe ó mhaith
a thiomáin an créatúr ina ruaill
tré duibheagán an uafáis

Níl eití ag an míol mór. Breathnaíonn cailín uirthi féin

Cad é an guairneán fomhuireach as a dtáinig an mhíol mór?
Déanann an cailín miongháire:

'As mo shamlaíocht féin   a uaisle   as mo shamhlaíocht féin'

Bladhm (1998)

MARÍA DO CEBREIRO

and

CAITRÍONA O'REILLY

Irish Translation by
RITA KELLY

A memoria é o espazo da reapropiación...

A memoria é o espazo da reapropiación.
Vivo para contalo. Gardo todas as fotos
para as que me pediron que sorrira.
Agora me decato de que endexamais prescindín
do trazo, da impiedade.
Porque a caligrafía consiste na ilusión de que non nos torcemos.
Nin os cadernos rubio darían ocultado
que o carbón mancha a pel
e que a mina se crava con frecuencia no páncreas do inimigo.
Agás no teu. Arrincáronche os ollos e iso faite inmortal.
(Entón ela abateuse prostrándose por terra e díxolle:
—por que atopei benquerencia aos teus ollos
para reparares en min,
sendo como son
unha estranxeira?)

o estadio do espello (1998)

Memory Is a Circumscribed Space...

Memory is a circumscribed space
and I alone am its witness. I have kept all the shots
in which I was required to smile.
All the time I was shadowed by impiety,
marked by the belief that I must not twist or turn.
No guide to pure line can obscure
the traces left on my skin
or the lead lodged in my enemy's gut.
But not in yours.
Your wounding makes you perfect in my eyes.

(then she fell at his feet and cried
Why is it I crave your regard
knowing I am a stranger to you?)

the mirror stage (1998)

A Terra Devastada

E aquela foi a única experiencia
que non puido escribir.
Así pasa coas últimas.
Pero tiña unha imprenta, e moito antes
compoñía os poemas coas súas mans.
A terra devastada, por exemplo,
ía callando lenta nos seus dedos.
Aquel torrón de herba
caeu dentro da folla e dela non saíu
nada que fose fresco,
ou verde coma os corpos
ao caer sobre os corpos.
Ela compuxo o texto coas súas mans
e os caracteres móbiles
deixáronlle saber que ese poema
caería no mundo como caen as árbores
ao paso azul do trono.
Un taboleiro ouija, aquela imprenta.
A equinácea curáballe o catarro á señora Sosostris
e os mortos besbellaban
"si" ou "non".
Foron aparecendo diante dela,
os que T. S. chamara
para que lle deixaran escribir
e o insomnio desfixese
aquel fero martelo de palabras.
Ou sería un castelo?
Iso pensa Virginia, pero non se confunde.
Os dedos case nunca se confunden.

Non queres que o poema te coñeza (2004)

The Waste Land

The last experience defeated her.
That she could not approach.
But she had a printing press
and for many years she had
built poems with her hands.
The Waste Land appeared under her touch,
a catalogue of truncated desires:
even she could not coax greenness
from those dead leaves.
So she constructed the thing by hand,
manipulating the characters
which told her the poem
would collide with the world
like a felled tree,
with the voice of thunder.
The press was a Ouija board
for Madame Sosostris and her sort—
neurasthenics in bangles and silks
through whom the dead murmur.
She can hear the hanged man he invoked
speaking to her in the voice of a bird.
It will not let her sleep.
Only her sensitive fingers can say
what kind of edifice they have made.

You Don't Want the Poem to Know You (2004)

Lúa

—Os músicos non son de ningún sitio.

Na habitación do hotel observa
os calcañares, o revés
do seu corpo. —Por que
non te descalzas?
Quero ver o que pasa cando tocas.

Faleille do veciño: —Cres
que lle doen os labios?
—Eu non toco a trompeta.
—Ven aquí.

Detense nas feridas.
—Son cicatrices? —Non.
A pel vólvese dura
pero quedan
as marcas. —Son pregos?
—Non me doen.

Achégase á ventá. A señora do baixo
baleira o cubo diante do portal.
—Hai meses que non chove.
O chan está moi seco, parece que ten
sede. —Queres ver como se abre?

—O deterxente non é un río.

Ás veces tarda días en facer as maletas.
—As cidades, os coches,
as horas que toquei.

Non se pode dicir que estivésemos xuntos.
(A contaminación, as diferenzas.)

Moon

"Musicians are citizens of nowhere."

In the darkened hotel room
I eyed his heels, the length of his smooth back.
"Take your shoes off.
Show me how you play."

We talked about the neighbour.
"Do you think his lips hurt?"
"How would I know?
I'm not a trumpeter."
"Come here."

He pulls up short at my wounds.
"What are these? Scars?" "No."
The skin has thickened
but still I am marked.
"Wrinkles then?"
"Never mind. I can't feel anything."

I go to the window. The downstairs neighbour
empties a bucket in her yard.
"It hasn't rained for months.
How scorched the earth is, how parched."
"Come, see how it opens."

"Detergent is hardly a river"
His dry laugh.

Sometimes it takes him weeks to pack his bags
—so many cities, cars, smoky bars.

We are too close, too distant
ever to be together.

—E despois que fixestes?
—Onde a pel se concentra é coma un vello,
se lle acaricio os pés teño a impresión
de que podo tocar toda a súa vida.
—Preguntácheslle algo?
—As cicatrices son o seu silencio.
(Os calcañares son o seu traballo.)
—É vulnerable ao tacto. Non é humilde.

Díxome: —Abre a ventá.

Confunde a súa imaxinación coa súa memoria.

Os hemisferios (2006)

126

"What happened afterwards?"
"I rubbed his feet—
feeling the calluses like an old man's,
touching the tender parts of his life."

"The scars are like closed mouths,"
they mark his silence.
My lover is easy to touch.
He is not humble.

Why do I confound memory and desire?

The Hemispheres (2006)

X.

Os dous tiñamos por veces
o rostro do sangue, ou sexa,
ningún rostro.
Non é doado comunicarse así,
mais tampouco é preciso.
Abonda con falar en voz moi baixa,
sen articulacións,
como se un de nós
(por exemplo,
a muller)
estivese suspendida no aire,
sen fío ningún,
e o outro
(un home, por exemplo)
estivese na auga
pero sen aboiar
e con todo
o son chegase enteiro á superficie.
Todos os sons.
Ningunha letra.
X.

Cuarto de outono (2008)

X.

Uaireanta, bhí aghaidheanna
Fuilseacha orainn, d'fhéadfá a rá,
Gan aghaidh.
Níl sé easca cumarsáid mar seo a bheith eadrainn,
Ní gá é ach an oiread.
Is leor labhairt i nguth an-séimh
Gan na focail a cheangail as a chéile,
Dá mba duine dhínn
(an bhean, mar shampla)
Crochta san aer
Gan téad,
Is an duine eile
(an fear, mar shampla)
San uisce
Gan snámh dá laghad
Ach fós
Tagann an fhuaim uile go ceannaghaidh
Na fuaimeanna go léir
Gan litir nó aibítir
X.

Autumn Room (2008)

The Death of Lieutenant General Sir John Moore. 1809

Para Paulino Vázquez

Unha parte do exército inglés, xunto co marqués de La Romana, sae cara a
Vigo perseguido polos militares franceses e logra embarcar, mentres o exército
galego regresa ao sur de Ourense e Moore se dirixe cara a Vigo seguido por
Soult. O paso do Manzanal e do Cebreiro en tempo de neve foi un
verdadeiro suplicio para ambos os dous bandos.

Un poema de fontes, documentos,
alma con lingua, ritmo, verso
longo. Un poema de heroes. Non
heroico. O sangue quente a arfar
pola chaqueta abaixo. Pequenos
botóns de ouro. Xenerais e bandeiras.
Pero as xustas. E non por evitar
o patriotismo, senón por concentrarse
no que importa. Aire que as fai tremer.
A feitura das nubes onde soñara Moore
un corpo novo. María Bertorini,
que non foi soterrada cabo
da súa amiga. Corunna
and the heights on which the battle
was fought. Non fago este poema
para que a ti che guste. Eu ben sei
(aquí ris) que estes dous versos de antes
te espantaron. E con todo, consólate
pensando que este non é o primeiro
que che debo. Igual que un agasallo
retrata a vaidade de quen dá
e di pouco de aquel a quen honramos.
Igual que aquela roda da santa
alexandrina no pórtico da praza
non fala do poder, senón da fame.

The Death of Lieutenant General Sir John Moore. 1809

For Paulino Vázquez

One part of the British army, together with the Marquis of La Romana, departs towards Vigo chased by the French military and manages to board, while the Galician army returns to the south of Ourense and Moore goes towards Vigo followed by Soult. In the season of snow, the Manzanal and Cebreiro passes were torture for both sides.

A poem of the source,
rising from darkness,
pulsing through verse. A poem for heroes,
yet not heroic. Blood,
still hot, spurts down a jacket,
reddens its gold buttons.
Generals; flags: such symbols.
Not to shun patriotism,
but to concentrate on what matters.
Air striking the bones like flint.
The massiveness of clouds where Moore
dreamt of a new body. María Bertorini,
who was not buried with her friend.
Corunna and the heights
on which the battle was fought.
I am not writing this poem to please you.
I know (I can hear you laugh)
that the two earlier verses appalled you.
But console yourself with the thought
that I am in your debt.
Rather, this is a gift which flatters no-one,
not even its giver.
It contains nothing of you.
In the same way the wheel in the portico,
the wheel of the Alexandrian martyr,

Este é un poema histórico
pero tamén un chisco *lady-like*,
onde caben os brillos entre a pedra,
as notas de Cornide sobre a ría,
a frescura do colo de Edith Swanehals,
a tumba de María
Mariño no Caurel,
un cartel que dicía só "Parada"
nunha tipografía que ao mellor
quixeras ver impresa na cuberta
do teu próximo libro. A neve
das montañas a interromper o paso
dos guerreiros, onde viven
os versos que aínda non escribiches
e os lugares sensibles do meu corpo.
Ou nas unllas da dona soñada por John Moore,
un plano da batalla, pero esta vez
sen morte. A pintura das unllas
poida que tamén debas desculpala.
O problema é nacer para vivir nun cuarto
e que a vida te leve a conquistar o mundo.
(Bernard Cassen: na loita
o primeiro en morrer é a verdade.)
Poetas e soldados. A estrela da mañá
volveu da fronte ao bico
e fixose xustiza aínda que tarde.
As guerras nunca son contemporáneas.
Ningunha cousa de ouro permanece.

Poemas históricos (unpublished)

tells nothing of power, only of terrible hunger.
This is a historical poem
but it is also a little chi-chi
with glints among the brickwork,
the mumsiness of Edith Swanehals' lap,
the tomb of María Mariño in the Caurel,
a sign that said only 'Parada'
in a fashionable font.
The heavy snowfalls in the mountains
blocking the soldiers' route
are like your unwritten verses,
or the parts of my body which remain untouched.
Or like the fingernails of the woman dreamed by John Moore,
reflecting the battle in their high polish,
only this time without death.
The problem is being born to live in one room
when what is in you wants to conquer the world.
(Bernard Cassen: the first casualty of war is truth)
Poets and soldiers. The morning star
declines from the brow of the hill
to the lips and Justice speaks:
War tarnishes. Nothing renews.
Nothing gold can stay.

Historical Poems (unpublished)

MARÍA LADO

and

MÁIGHRÉAD MEDBH

Irish Translation by
RITA KELLY

así doe novembro.
así doen as moas apretadas contra ti, coma un barco,
unha traxedia para un pobo
ou o recordo dun membro fantasma. doe
porque non te das ido aínda que marcharas,
e non hai bálsamos para o baleiro dun amputado.
nin sequera doses xustificadas de codeína
contestan as miñas mensaxes.
nunca preguntas.
por min. nunca preguntas por min.
así doe a praia na que nos coñecemos.
toda ela cábeme espesa nos petos do abrigo
e entérranse as mans entre as cunchiñas, facéndome cortes.
sabes que sangro polas mañáns?
pequenos cortes invisibles que deixou todo o que vén despois da marea.
así doe novembro,
e máis.
inmenso.
onde o mar rompe contra as rochas
novembro doe inmenso.
alí é onde máis manca
que non che sexa
nin sequera un recordo.

nove (2008)

136

how november hurts
how my molars hurt, ground against you like a boat,
how a national tragedy hurts
or the haunting memory of a limb. it hurts
because you may start out, but you'll never leave,
and there's no medicine for the ghosts of an amputee.
not even the warranted codeine pills
answer my messages.
you never enquire.
about me. you never enquire about me.
how the beach hurts, where we first met.
it's all here, packed in the pockets of my coat
and my hands bury themselves in the small, slicing shells.
do you know that I bleed in the mornings?
tiny, unseen cuts left by the jetsam of the tide.
this is how november hurts,
and more.
fathomless.
where sea collides with rock
november hurts fathomless.
but where it cruelly cripples
is that nothing can make you
remember.

nine (2008)

no cabo máis occidental da costa
rompen as mareas de máis encher
e a illa é a penas unha pedra na que morde o mar.
hai que fixarse moito porque ata a paisaxe é enganosa, xira
leva ese aire lento de balea.
e vai desaparecendo debaixo das ondas.

na illa sábeno e chaman a esta rexión mínima
novembro
porque é cruel coma un amante.

saben que os cormoráns vixían aos homes.
intentan evitar que fuxan envoltos nas mortallas dos ausentes.
e amárranos á terra con cordas que non se ven.

a marea sofre. e desfaise en espuma por dar con elas.
e danlle ese nome por iso.

porque aquí é onde veñen parar os cargueiros que engule o mar.
e os fardos arrastrados co seu peso de mortos.
chegan ata as furnas onde se esconden os mellores percebes
e aniñan entre eles.
alí agardan polos dedos cegos dos homes.
cóllenos polas mans para que o mar os aperte.

todos na illa o saben.
novembro é o lugar onde o mar desexa a carne.
sabe os nosos nomes íntimos

e é por iso que os **percebes** enganan con voces de serea.

nove (2008)

138

where the world ends on the western cape,
there break the ravenous tides,
chewing the island to a stone.
pay attention, because the landscape is a trickster, shifting,
becoming the slow turn of a whale,
vanishing piece by piece beneath the waves.

the islanders know it and they call this bitten place
november,
for it is savage as a lover.

they know the cormorants are guarding the men.
so they don't go shrouded in the forms of the missing,
they lash them to land with invisible ropes.

the tide aches. leaps to claim them in a rage of spume.
they call it november.

because this is where the guzzling sea throws up its boats.
the cargo too, hauled by their dead weight.
they lodge in hoarding grottoes of the treasured percebes
and nest there.
waiting for the blind fingers of men.
snatching them away to the arms of the sea.

everyone on the island knows.
november is the place where sea seeks flesh.
it has learned our secret names

and **percebes** sing them like sirens.

TRANSLATOR'S NOTE: 'Percebes' are gooseneck barnacles, a delicacy in Galicia.

nine (2008)

se acaso os soños as visitan,
é **ritual** das mulleres máis novas da illa
convocar aos que alí moran en lugar abrigado.
e para aviso
á porta de cada casa
sinais en segredo que codifican a cita.
e que poden ser lirios,
semprevivas, acivros ou gardenias,
que deitadas desta ou outra maneira
indican o lugar exacto
onde relatarán o soñado con precisión de detalles.

é ritual das mulleres
porque as súas mans coñecen as redes.
e é só con eses aparellos
que se pode ter conta das palabras.

pero non é tan sinxelo.
cando as mulleres soñan
as gaivotas son enviadas polas tempestades.
en poucos segundos,
exércitos excitados de aves cobren o ceo.

esa é a verdade.

despois fan os niños sobre as casas daquelas que aínda son fértiles
e enmarañan os seus berros nos tellados.

ningunha outra cousa se escoita.
durmir é imposible.
as lúas non chegan a encher.
as mareas nunca abalan ata calmar.
e a falta de descanso arruína tamén os nacementos.

esa é a verdade,
todo se vira
contra os habitantes da desesperada.

nove (2008)

if they are visited by desires,
the youngest women of the island **ritually**
convene the sheltering dwellers.
and to let them know,
secret signs encode the date
on the door of each house.
it could be irises,
houseleeks, holly, gardenias,
that, set at certain angles,
show exactly the place
where all will be told, in painstaking detail.

it is a women's ritual,
because they weave the nets.
and it is only these nets
that can harvest the words.

but it's not that simple.
when the women desire,
seagulls are sent by tempestuous winds.
in a few seconds,
frenzied feathered armies steal the sky.

i swear it's true.

later, they nest on the homes of the fertile,
meshing their cries into the eaves.

nothing else can be heard.
not a hope of sleep.
the moon will not swell to the full.
nor the tide ebb to its ease.
without rest, how can there be birth?

i swear it's true.
the whole world turns
against these dwellers on the desperate.

nine (2008)

cuqui é pequeno de máis para ser un osiño de peluxe
e cáelle o nariz
por iso non lle gusta ir á lavadora
nin que mamá o colgue a secar polas orellas
ademais
bótame de menos durante o centrifugado
    e eu a el   ¿ e se lle doe?
    as orellas   ¿e se lle doen as orellas das pinzas?
    ou estar só tanto tempo na trandeira

e eu a el   sobre todo hoxe que é luns e ti estás tan lonxe
así que o meto húmido debaixo das sabas
e apértoo
para que non chore máis que eu sexa xa grande
que me gusta   porque sei que me quere pequeno
como só poden querer os osiños os nenos
que lles perdoan ata a dor das pinzas

como sei que ti e eu nos queremos

casa atlántica, casa cabaret (2001)

Tá **cuqui** ró-bheag bheith ina bhéirín líonta
Is tá a shróinín ag titim dhe
Mar sin níl dúil dá laghad aige san inneall níocháin
Nó sa chaoi ina chrochann Mam é óna chluasa le triomú
Lena cois sin, airíonn sé mise uaidh le linn an chasadh lártheifnigh
Agus airím uaim é   agus má ghoilleann sé é?
A chluasa   agus má ghoilleann sé a chluasa
Leis na diabhail pionnaí éadaigh sin?
Agus bheith ina aonar chomh fada sin ar an raca triomaithe.

Is braithim uaim é go háirithe inniu, Dé Luain, is tusa
        chomh fada sin i gcéin uaim
Mar sin cuirim ina luí é, fós tais, faoi na h-éadaí leapa
Cuachaim le m'ucht é
Ionas nach ritheann an deor leis toisc go bhfuilim fásta suas anois
Is aoibhinn liom é mar tá fhios agam gur mhaith leis dá mbeinn
        arís i mo thachrán
Mar ní féidir leis an mbéirín grá a dháileadh ar éinne seachas leannaí
Maitheann sé fiú fulaingt na bpionnaí éadaigh

Mar tá fhios agam go bhfuil tusa is mise i ngrá le chéile.

teach atlantach, teach pléaráca (2001)

143

inventei **bonaval** e a nosa cama
estaba chea de flores,
así
claro que non tiña medo dos nichos
e agradecía que anoitecese entre os teus brazos
e as estrelas co seu canto de grilos
quería dicirche:
delicioso
é como se escribe
o teu nome baixo as árbores.

berlín (2005)

i conjured **bonaval** and our bed
burst into flower
so bright
i could no longer fear the burial niches
but welcomed night rising in your arms
and the air starry with cricketsong
i wanted to tell you:
delicious
is the name
i have given you under the trees.

TRANSLATOR'S NOTE: Bonaval is a popular park in the city of Santiago de Compostela.

berlin (2005)

XIANA ARIAS

and

PADDY BUSHE

Este é o lugar onde medra a morte...

Este é o lugar onde medra a morte.
Médranlle as mans á morte
para agarrarte mellor.
Deixa de andar ás carreiras,
aí vén o sol e trae sombras.

Emborráchate, para que te emborrachas.
Báixate, súbete ao carro do supermercado
ata que se acaben todas as estradas do mundo.

Pero anda dereita, ponte dereita.
Non andes arrastrando os pés.

"Cleo de dez a doce" (2007)

Here Is the Place of Death's Growing...

Here is the place of death's growing.
The hands of death grow
to grip you well.
Have done with that mad rush,
see, the sun comes, bearing shadows.

Drunk, and for what?
Get down, settle yourself on the shopping trolley
until all the ways of the world meet.

But go upright, stand upright.
Do not drag your feet as you go.

"Cleo from Ten to Twelve" (2007)

Non hai pistolas...

Non hai pistolas.
—Cando imos saír desta cidade?

Non hai chisqueiros.
—Falar contigo é como discutir coa televisión.

Non teño un mapa.
—Se a porta pechada é a tranquilidade... que medo!

Acusación (2009)

There Are No Guns...

There are no guns.
—When do we abandon this city?

There are no lighters.
—To speak to you is to squabble with the television.

I have no map.
—If tranquillity means a closed door ... the dread!

Accusation (2009)

Recoñézome na dor...

Recoñézome na dor:

Non foi fácil ir ás festas.
Á volta pasabamos días
e noites enteiras atadas
ás patas da cama.

Non eramos lobas
pero tiñamos fame.

Acusación (2009)

Aithním mé Féin sa bhFulaingt...

Aithním mé féin sa bhfulaingt:

Níorbh éasca dul go dtí na cóisir.
Ag filleadh dúinn chaithimis laethanta
agus oícheanta iomlána ceangailte
ag cosa na leaba.

Ní faolchúnna a bhí ionainn
ach bhíomar stiúgtha.

Gearán (2009)

Sentada na porta da casa...

Sentada na porta da casa,
cun coxín na barriga,
cara de poucos amigos
e así se pasou maio.
Cumpríndolle os antollos.
O médico díxolle que tiña un embarazo psicolóxico.
Aos nove meses pariu un cartón de tabaco.

Ortigas (2007)

By the Door of Her House, Sitting...

By the door of her house, sitting
with a cushion to her belly,
her face unfriendly:
thus May passed by.
Indulging herself.
A hysterical pregnancy, the doctor said.
Nine months later she had a carton of cigarettes.

Stinging Nettles (2007)

Isto non é literatura feminina...

Isto non é literatura feminina, dixo mentres escribía unha obra de teatro para nenos. Hai un guerreiro que rescata unha muller fermosa dos brazos dun home malvado. Ao final ela vaise, soa, cravando as unllas dos pés no asfalto.

Ortigas (2007)

This Is Not Feminine Literature...

This is not feminine literature, the author said, while writing a play for children. There is a hero who snatches a beautiful woman from the arms of an evil man. In the end she leaves, alone, scoring the asphalt with her toenails.

Stinging Nettles (2007)

ABOUT THE POETS

By *María Xesús Nogueira and Laura Lojo*

MARILAR ALEIXANDRE was born in Madrid in 1947 and has lived in Galicia since 1973. She was part of the *Batallón Literario da Costa da Morte*, a group that was an energetic contributor to the poetry scene in the late 1990s. She holds a doctorate in Biology and teaches in the Science Education Department at the University of Santiago de Compostela. Galician has been the language of her literary creations from the start, and she works in various genres: children's and juvenile fiction, adult fiction—for which she has won several prizes—and poetry. Her first book of poems, *Catálogo de velenos* [Catalogue of Poisons] (Ferrol: Sociedade de Cultura Valle-Inclán, 1999) won the Esquío Poetry Prize. She later published *Desmentindo a primavera* [Denying Spring] (Vigo: Xerais, 2003), *Abecedario das árbores* [ABC of Trees](Santiago: Grupo Correo Gallego/Concello de Santiago, 2006) and *Mudanzas* [Shiftings] (Santiago: Danú/PEN Clube de Galicia, 2007), which was awarded the Caixanova Poetry Prize. Her work as a literary translator was honoured in 2009 on International Translation Day.

XIANA ARIAS was born in Fonsagrada in the province of Lugo in 1983, and has published two books of poems to date, *Ortigas* [Stinging Nettles] (A Coruña: Espiral Maior, 2007), winner of the Xosé María Pérez Parallé National Poetry Prize, and *Acusación* [Accusation] (Vigo: Galaxia, 2009). A journalist, she currently works for the programme "Diario Cultural" on Radio Galega. She participates frequently in poetry publications and reading events.

PADDY BUSHE is a prize-winning poet both in Irish and English. He was born in Dublin in 1948, and now lives in Waterville, Co. Kerry. He has published eight collections of poetry, the most recent of which is *To Ring in Silence: New and Selected Poems* (Dublin: Dedalus Press, 2008), a bilingual volume with a foreword by Bernard O'Donoghue. Other work includes *Digging Towards the Light* (Dedalus, 1994), *Hopkins on Skellig Michael* (Dedalus, 2001), and *The Nitpicking of Cranes* (Dedalus, 2005).

Widely involved in cultural activities in Ireland, he has directed the Strokestown International Poetry Festival, and has also published three books of translation from Irish, Scottish Gaelic and Chinese, as well as translating many individual poems. The recipient of the Oireachtas prize for poetry in 2006, Paddy Bushe was also the recipient of the 2006 Michael Hartnett Poetry Award.

CELIA DE FRÉINE is a poet, playwright, librettist and screenwriter who writes in Irish and English. She has published four collections of poetry: *Faoi Chabáistí is Ríonacha* (Cló Iar-Chonnachta, 2001), *Fiacha Fola* (Cló Iar-Chonnachta, 2004), *Scarecrows at Newtownards* (Scotus Press, 2005) and *imram: odyssey* (Arlen House, 2010). Her poetry has won many awards, including the Patrick Kavanagh Award (1994) and Gradam Litríochta Chló Iar-Chonnachta (2004). In 2009 Arlen House published *Mná Dána*, a collection of plays, each of which had won an Oireachtas award. The same year the Abbey Theatre presented a rehearsed reading of her short play *Casadh* which it had commissioned. Films, written by her, have been shown in festivals in Ireland and the United States. Further information: www.celiadefreine.com

MAURICE HARMON has a long-established reputation as an academic and poet. His published academic work includes *Sean O'Faolain: A Critical Study* (Notre Dame, IN: U. of Notre Dame P., 1966); *The Poetry of Thomas Kinsella* (Dublin: Wolfhound, 1974); *Irish Poetry After Yeats: Seven Poets* (Dublin, Wolfhound, 1979); *Thomas Kinsella: Designing for the Exact Needs* (Dublin: Irish Academic Press, 2008); *Select Bibliography for the Study of Anglo-Irish Literature and Its Backgrounds* (Portland: PD Meany, 1977); *Austin Clarke 1896-1974: A Critical Introduction* (London: Merlin Press, 1998); *No Author Better Served: The Correspondence between Samuel Beckett and Alan Schneider* (Cambridge, MA: Harvard U.P., 1998); and *The Colloquy of the Old Men* (Palo Alto, CA: Academica Press, 2001)—Harmon's translation of *Acallam na Senorach*, the medieval compendium of stories and poems. In 2006, Irish Academic Press published his *Selected Essays*, edited by Barbara Brown. His poetry collections include *The Last Regatta, Selected Poems 1988-2000* (Cliffs of Moher: Salmon, 2000), *The Doll with Two Backs* (Salmon, 2004); and *The Mischievous Boy* (Salmon, 2008).

ANNE LE MARQUAND HARTIGAN is a poet, painter, essayist and playwright who moves beyond the conventional limits of both visual image and written word. She constantly engages the reader in a series of questions, reflections, reformulations, and perceptions, while the poems convey enormous humanity which is unsentimental and often uncompromising and witty. Hartigan has published six collections: *Long Tongue* (Dublin: Beaver Row Press, 1982), *Return Single* (Beaver Row Press, 1986), *Now is a Moveable Feast* (Bridge Mills, Galway: Salmon, 1991),

Immortal Sins (Galway: Salmon, 1993), *Nourishment* (Cliffs of Moher, Co. Clare: Salmon, 2005), and *To Keep the Light Burning: Reflections in times of loss* (Salmon, 2008). She is also the author of seven plays: *Beds* (1982), *La Corbière* (1989), *Jersey Lilies: A Trilogy* (1996) and *The Secret Game* (1995), which won her the prestigious Mobil Prize for Playwriting. One play was commissioned and performed by Ohio Northern University in 2003 and at the Edinburgh Festival, and Otago University, New Zealand produced another. One of her pervading themes addresses the place of the female artist in society, and the challenges and difficulties encountered in bringing artistic work to realisation. In 1996 Hartigan wrote an influential essay entitled *Clearing the Space: A Why of Writing* (Salmon, 1996).

RITA KELLY was born in Galway, Ireland. Kelly has extensively published poetry, narrative, criticism and a play. Along with her late husband, the poet Eoghan Ó Tuairisc, she wrote *Dialann sa Díseart* (Dublin: Coiscéim, 1981), a collection of lyric meditations on nature. Kelly has published the poetry collections *An Bealach Éadóigh* (Coiscéim, 1984), *Fare Well/Beir Beannacht* (Dublin: Attic Press, 1990), Travelling West (Dublin: Arlen House, 2000), and *Turas go Bun na Spéire* (Conamara: Cló Iar-Chonnachta, 2009). She is also the author of *The Whispering Arch and Other Stories* (Arlen House, 1986), *Kelly Reads Bewick* (Arlen House, 2001) and the play *Frau Luther* (1984). Kelly has won the Irish Times/Merriman Poetry Award (1975), The Sean O'Riordain Memorial Prize for Poetry (1980), The Katherine & Patrick Kavanagh Memorial Award (2007) and was awarded three Arts Council/An Chomhairle Éalaíon Bursaries for Literature.

MARÍA DO CARME KRUCKENBERG was born in Vigo in 1926. An incessant traveller, her life has been shared between Argentina and her native city, where she currently lives. In Buenos Aires, she came into contact with Galician and Spanish intellectuals exiled for political reasons, and with many South American writers. Her first quarter century of poetic production, at first in Castilian then in Galician, is gathered in *Obra poética case completa* [1953-2000] [The Nearly Complete Poetic Work] (Sada, A Coruña: Ediciós do Castro, 2000). Since then, she has published *Lembranzas da beleza triste* [Memories of Sad Beauty](A Coruña: Espiral Maior, 2003), *Luz para un novo amencer* [Light for New Dawn] (Sada, A Coruña: Ediciós do Castro, 2004), *As complexas mareas da noite* [The Complex Tides of the Night] (A Coruña: Espiral Maior, 2006) and *Os límites do arreguizo* [Shiver's Limits] (A Coruña: Espiral Maior, 2008). She has been awarded many prizes, including the Alecrín Prize (1997) and the Medalla de Galicia (1998).

MARÍA LADO was born in Cee in the province of A Coruña in 1979. She was in the Batallón Literario da Costa da Morte [Literary Battalion of Costa da Morte] and has worked in the audiovisual field and in puppet theatre. Her books: *A primeira visión* [First Vision] (A Mahía: Letras de Cal, 1997), *casa atlántica, casa cabaré* [atlantic house, cabaret house] (Vigo: Xerais, 2001), *berlín* (Santiago de Compostela: Grupo Correo Gallego/Concello de Santiago, 2005) e *nove* [nine] (A Estrada: Edicións Fervenza, 2008), which won the Avelina Valladares Poetry Prize. She writes the blog *Casa atlántica* and lately mixes music and new technologies in the performance and broadcast of her poetry. Her personal symbology revolves around childhood, experience, and maritime landscape.

Poet and novelist CATHERINE PHIL MacCARTHY was born in Limerick and educated at University College Cork, Trinity College Dublin and The Central School of Speech and Drama, London. Joint winner, with Susan Connolly, of the Poetry Ireland and Sense of Place Award in 1991, a selection of her poems was also published in *How High the Moon*. In her second, critically well-received collection *This Hour of the Tide* (Cliffs of Moher, Co. Clare: Salmon, 1994), MacCarthy—with characteristic subtlety and attention to the aesthetics of poetry—explores landscape filtered through the lens of a feeling imagination. She is also the author of *The Blue Globe* (Belfast: Blackstaff Press, 1998) and *Suntrap* (Blackstaff, 2007), where the scenario of her Irish country childhood powerfully combines with subversive eroticism and grace-filled individual experience. Her aesthetic is patiently explored, and her voice insists on authenticity. MacCarthy's reviewers have emphasised that her debut novel *One Room Everywhere* (Blackstaff, 2003) is a surprising exploration of love and desire.

MARY O'MALLEY was born in Connemara and educated at University College, Galway. She spent many years living in Portugal before returning to Ireland in the late 1980s and beginning a poetry career in 1990 with the title *A Consideration of Silk* (Galway: Salmon, 1990). O'Malley has since published six other books *Where the Rocks Float* (Salmon, 1993), *The Knife in the Wave* (Cliffs of Moher, Co. Clare: Salmon, 1997), *Asylum Road* (Salmon, 2001), *The Boning Hall: New and Selected Poems* (Manchester: Carcanet, 2002) and *A Perfect V* (Carcanet, 2006), all of them translated into several languages. O'Malley's poetry exceeds what has been traditionally accepted as poetic subject matters by addressing female complexity through her sexuality, the body, and daily routine. O'Malley's critical perspective also takes as its focal point Irish identity, and explores our response to recent immigration in the light of our own history, as best shown in her fourth collection of poetry *Asylum Road*. O'Malley's reviewers have often remarked on her ability to conjugate the particular and local with the universal and global through a web of evocative resonances. She received a Hennessey Award in 1990, a Lawrence O'Shaughnessy Award in 2009, and is a member of Aosdána.

MARÍA DO CEBREIRO was born in Santiago de Compostela in 1976. She holds a doctorate in Literary Theory and is a Lecturer at the University of Santiago de Compostela. She is also an essayist and researcher, and is active in Galician cultural life. Her first book of poetry appeared in the 1990s, *o estadio do espello* [the mirror stage] (Vigo: Xerais, 1998). Her next book, (*nós, as inadaptadas*) [we, the maladjusted women] (Ferrol: Sociedad de Cultura Valle Inclán, 2001, runner-up for the Esquío Poetry Prize) cast a feminist look at a classic essay by Vicente Risco, *Nós os inadaptados* (1933), reflecting a strategy frequently employed by the author, that of playful dialogue with cultural referents. Other titles: *Non queres que o poema te coñeza* [You Don't Want the Poem to Know You] (Santiago: Danú/PEN Clube de Galicia, 2004), which won the Caixanova Poetry Prize, *O barrio das chinesas* [Chinatown (in the feminine)] (Santiago: Grupo Correo Gallego/Concello de Santiago, 2005), *Os hemisferios* [The Hemispheres] (Vigo: Galaxia, 2006), *Cuarto de outono* [Autumn Room] (Santiago: Sotelo Blanco, 2008) and *Non son de aquí* [I Am Not From Here] (Vigo: Xerais, 2008), which has appeared in English in 2010 from Shearsman Books in Exeter, UK.

MÁIGHRÉAD MEDBH was born in Newcastle West, Co. Limerick. Her debut collection of poetry was entitled *The Making of a Pagan* (Belfast: Blackstaff Press, 1990). Medbh's poetry explores the vicissitudes of a difficult childhood and the socio-political environment in lines where formal design matches individual experience. The conviction that poetry emerges from one's body led her to experiment with musical rhythms, and moved her towards performance poetry. A second collection of poetry, *Tenant* (Cliffs of Moher, Co. Clare: Salmon, 1999), is a narrative sequence which centres on a fictitious family during the Famine years. It explores physical hunger as well as hunger for self-expression, subjectivity and national identity. *Split* (in *iDivas!*, Galway: Arlen House, 2003) delves into questions of individuality and relationship. In 2009, *When the Air Inhales You* was published by Arlen House. A mix of themes and styles in the first part of this collection leads into Part 2, which is a requiem in twenty-two short poems. The outstanding performance poet of her generation, she is a unique presence in the Irish literary scene. Further information: www.maighreadmedbh.ie

NUALA NÍ DHOMHNAILL is widely acknowledged as one of contemporary Ireland's greatest poets, also reputed for her dedication and defence of the Irish language. Ní Dhomhnaill has published extensively and her works include poetry collections, children's plays, screenplays, anthologies, articles, reviews and essays. In her writings, Ní Dhomhnaill focuses on the rich traditions and heritage of Ireland, and draws upon themes of ancient Irish folklore and mythology that intermingle with contemporary issues concerning femininity, sexuality and culture. In

1981, Ní Dhomhnaill published her fist poetry collection, *An Dealg Droighin* (Cork: Mercier Press), and became a member of Aosdána. Other works include *Féar Suaithinseach* (Maynooth: An Sagart, 1984); *Feis* (An Sagart, 1991), and *Cead Aighnis* (also translated by Eiléan Ní Chuilleanáin and Medbh McGuckian; Gallery Press, 2002 and Wake Forest University Press, 2000). Ní Dhomhnaill's poems appeared in English translation in the dual-language editions *Rogha Dánta/Selected Poems* (Dublin: Raven Arts Press, 1986, 1988, 1990; translated by Michael Harnett); *The Astrakhan Cloak* (Oldcastle: Gallery translated by Paul Muldoon, 1991, 1992), *Pharaoh's Daughter* (Gallery, 1990), and *The Fifty Minute Mermaid* (translated by Paul Muldoon; Gallery, 2007).

MARTIN NUGENT was raised in County Offaly, and educated at Maynooth College, Co. Kildare, where he received a first class honours MA in Irish in 1983. He has published several works, including a handbook of daily phraseology in Irish, *Síolta* (Folens, 1981), *Drámaí Eoghain Uí Thuairisc* (An Sagart, 1984) and *Léas* (Folens, 1994), also criticism in Irish newspapers and journals. He has lectured at Maynooth and Galway universities, as well as at various Education Centres throughout Ireland. Today, he works as Assistant Headmaster in Clongowes Wood College, Co. Kildare.

CAITRÍONA O'REILLY was born in Dublin, and educated at Trinity College, Dublin. Her first poetry collection, *The Nowhere Birds* (Northumberland, UK: Bloodaxe, 2001) was awarded the Rooney Prize for Irish Literature and marked her early on as one of the most gifted poets of her generation. *The Nowhere Birds* sets off a journey from the very particular—the poet's childhood in Ireland—to encompass cosmopolitan experience in highly versatile poems. *The Sea Cabinet* (Bloodaxe, 2006) consolidated the achievement of O'Reilly's debut volume by enacting the dilemmas and concerns of individual conscience in a rapidly changing environment. Reviewers have often remarked that O'Reilly's highly-regarded poetry focuses on a precise observation of the natural order, which runs parallel to an individual journey through a surrealist landscape. O'Reilly's powers of observation apply also to the field of literary criticism: she was a contributing editor of the Irish poetry journal *Metre*, collaborated with artist Isabel Nolan, and was editor of *Poetry Ireland Review* during 2009.

CHUS PATO was born in Ourense in 1955. She holds a degree in History and Geography and teaches at the secondary school level. One of the most esteemed voices in contemporary literature, she is a member of Redes Escarlata [Scarlet Networks], a cultural and social network created in 2001 by nationalist and leftist intellectuals. Her poetry appeared in various anthologies before her first book, *Urania* (Ourense: Calpurnia, 1991) was published. Her next books were *Heloísa* (A Coruña: Espiral

Maior, 1994), *Fascinio* [Fascination] (Muros: Toxosoutos, 1995), *A ponte das poldras* [Stepping Stone Bridge] (Santiago: Noitarenga, 1996) and *Nínive* [Nineveh] (Vigo: Xerais, 1996, Losada Diéguez Prize). Critics agree that *m-Talá* (Vigo: Xerais, 2000) marks an inflection point in her poetry and a turn toward a hybridization of textual typologies and a radically innovative aesthetic. The book is the first in the pentalogy titled *Method*, and was followed by *Charenton* (Vigo: Xerais, 2004), *Hordas de escritura* [Hordes of Writing] (Vigo: Xerais, 2008, Spanish Critics' Prize) and *Secesión* [Secession] (Vigo: Galaxia, 2009). The destruction of syntax and elaboration of a political discourse are two constants in Chus Pato's poetry. Her work is present in anthologies of Galician poetry of recent years, and *Charenton* and *m-Talá* have appeared in English translation (Exeter: Shearsman, 2007 and 2009), with *Hordes of Writing* forthcoming in 2010.

LUZ PICHEL, born in Alén in the province of Pontevedra in 1947, has lived for many years in Madrid, where she taught Spanish language and literature at the secondary school level. She works with the Centre for Poetry Studies at the Universidad Popular José Hierro in San Sebastián de los Reyes (Madrid). After publishing several books in Spanish (*El pájaro mudo*, 1990; *La marca de los potros*, 2004; *El pájaro mudo y otros poemas*, 2004), she entered the Galician literary system with *Casa pechada* [Locked House] (Ferrol: Sociedad de Cultura Valle Inclán, 2006), which explores memories of childhood and origin, and won the Esquío Poetry Prize.

LUZ POZO GARZA was born in Ribadeo, in the province of Lugo, in 1922, and grew up on the Galician Cantabrian coast. As with many poets of her generation, she started writing in Spanish, but adopted Galician as her literary language in 1952 with the publication of *O paxaro na boca* [The Bird in the Mouth] (Lugo: Xistral, 1952). Other books: *Concerto de outono* [Autumn Concerto] (Sada, A Coruña: Ediciós do Castro, 1981), *Códice Calixtino* [Codex Calixtinus] (Barcelona: Sotelo Blanco, 1986), *Prometo a flor de loto* [I Promise the Lotus Flower] (A Coruña: Deputación Provincial 1992, Miguel González Garcés Poetry Prize), *Vida secreta de Rosalía* [Secret Life of Rosalía] (A Coruña: Espiral Maior, 1996), *Ribadeo, Ribadeo* (Ribadeo: Concello de Ribadeo, 2002), *As Arpas de Iwerddon* [The Harps of Iwerddon] (Ourense: Linteo, 2005)—a book with an Irish focus—and *Deter o día cunha flor* [Detaining the Day with a Flower] (A Coruña: Baía, 2009). Her selected poems have appeared as *Historias fidelísimas. Poesía selecta 1952-2003* [Keeping the Faith: Selected Poems 1952-2003] (Santiago: Danú/PEN Clube de Galicia, 2003) and *Memoria solar* [Solar Memory] (Ourense: Linteo, 2004). The natural world and love inspire a great part of her work. She taught Spanish language and literature and was editor of the poetry journals *Nordés* and *Clave Orión*. As well as poetry, she has written a play, *Medea en Corinto* [Medea in Corinth] (Ourense: Linteo, 2003), and an important body of critical work and essays. She is one of the few women invited to date to join the the Royal Galician Academy, and her inaugural speech was called "Diálogos con Rosalía" [Dialogues with Rosalía de Castro]. Her name was proposed in 2007 as candidate for the Nobel Prize for Literature.

ANA ROMANÍ was born in Noia, in the province of A Coruña, in 1962 and has been long active in the promotion of feminist ideas and of poetry. She works as a journalist for Radio Galega, where she has directed the program Diario Cultural for the past twenty years. Her work has been distinguished by several prizes, notably the First Irmandade do Libro Prize (1992), the Federación de Gremios de Editores de España Prize for encouraging reading—radio section—(2007), the Atlántida Prize for the radio journalist of the year from the Gremi de Editors de Catalunya (2008) and the Marisa Soto Prize from the Asociación de Actores e Actrices de Galicia (2008). Her trajectory in poetry began in the late 1980s with *Palabra de mar* [Seaword] (A Coruña: Espiral Maior, 1987), followed by *Das últimas mareas* [On the Last Tides] (A Coruña: Espiral Maior, 1994), *Arden* [Blazing] (A Coruña: Espiral Maior, 1998) and *Love me tender: 24 pezas mínimas para unha caixa de música* [Love Me Tender: 24 Minimal Pieces for a Music Box] (Santiago de Compostela: Grupo Correo Gallego/Concello de Santiago, 2005). Her poetry is characterized by a feminist reinscription of myths and a questioning of subjects. She has participated in many performances, including *O Son da Pedra* [Sound of Stone] (1994, with the musical group Milladoiro), *Ó outro extremo do paraíso* [The Other Side of Paradise] (1997) and *Lob@s* [S/he-Wolves] (1999, both with Antón Lopo, with whom she also created the Laboratorio de Indagacións Poéticas), *Son delas* [Women's Sounds] (2000, coordinated by the singer Uxía Senlle), *Estalactitas* [Stalactites] (2002, with poets Anxos Romeo and Lupe Gómez), *Catro poetas suicidas. Intervención poética contra a levidade* [Four Suicidal Poets: Poetic Intervention Against Levity] (2002) and *A voz e o poema. Os periplos de Avilés de Taramancos* [Voice and Poem: The Journeys of Avilés de Taramancos] (2003).

LORNA SHAUGHNESSY was born in Belfast and lives in Co. Galway. Her first collection of poetry, *Torching the Brown River* was published by Salmon Poetry in 2008. Her work was included in the Forward Book of Poetry 2009. She lectures in Spanish in the National University of Ireland, Galway, and has published two translations of contemporary Mexican poetry with Arlen House, *Mother Tongue. Selected Poems* by Pura López Colomé and *If We Have Lost Our Oldest Tales* (Fábula de los perdidos) by María Baranda. Her second collection of poems will be published by Salmon in 2011.

XOHANA TORRES was born in Santiago de Compostela in 1931. She has also lived in Ferrol and Vigo, two cities that significantly mark her poetry. She started publishing in the 1950s with the book of poems *Do sulco* [Furrow] (Vigo: Galaxia, 1957), followed by *Estacións ao mar* [Seasons to the Sea] (Vigo: Galaxia, 1980, Spanish Critics' Prize) and *Tempo de ría* [Estuary Time] (A Coruña: Espiral Maior, 1992). Her emblematic poem "Penelope", which appeared in *Tempo de ría*, has served as a reference point for the generations of women poets that have followed her. The feminine gaze evident in these texts is characteristic of the work of Xohana Torres, which also includes two plays, *Á outra banda do Iberr* [The Far Side of the Iberr] (Vigo: Galaxia, 1965) and *Un hotel de primeira sobre o río* [Posh Riverside Hotel] (Vigo: Galaxia, 1968) and the novel *Adiós María* (Vigo: Galaxia, 1970), in which the influence of the innovative fiction of the day left its mark. Also a pioneer in radio broadcasting in Galician in the post-civil-war era, she is a member of the Royal Galician Academy and the title of her inaugural discourse there, "Eu tamén navegar" [I Too Shall Navigate] remains a feminist and cultural rallying cry. Among her many prizes and distinctions, she has received the prestigious Pedrón de Ouro Prize in honour of her contributions to Galician culture.

★ Special thanks to MINIA BONGIORNO GARCÍA who undertook the translation into English of the Galician poems in this anthology, in order to orient the Irish poets in their versions. Bongiorno was born in New Orleans and raised in Connecticut. She received her BA in Spanish and French from Wellesley College (Wellesley, Massachusetts) in 1992. She went on to receive her MA (1995) and PhD degrees (2003) in Hispanic Studies from Brown University (Providence, Rhode Island), specialising in twentieth-century Spanish women's fiction. She served as a Lecturer in English at the University of Santiago de Compostela for several years while conducting her doctoral research. Since 2006, she is an English teacher in the Galician public secondary school system. Bongiorno is also a freelance translator in her spare time. She has collaborated in works such as *A tribo das baleas: poetas de arestora/An Anthology of the Latest Galician Poetry* (Vigo: Xerais, 2001), *Mans salgadas/Salty Hands* by Javier Teniente (Vigo: Xerais, 2002), and *Writing Bonds. Irish and Galician Contemporary Women Poets*, edited by Manuela Palacios and Laura Lojo (Oxford: Peter Lang, 2009).

ABOUT THE EDITORS

MARY O'DONNELL is a poet, short story writer and novelist who has been very active in Irish cultural affairs since the 1980s. A member of Aosdána and of the Irish Writers' Union and former member of the Governing Authority at NUI Maynooth, she has published six collections of poetry: *Reading the Sunflowers in September* (Galway: Salmon, 1990), *Spiderwoman's Third Avenue Rhapsody* (Galway: Salmon, 1993), *Unlegendary Heroes* (Cliffs of Moher, Co. Clare: Salmon, 1998), *September Elegies* (Belfast: Lapwing, 2003), *The Place of Miracles: New and Selected Poems* (Dublin: New Island Books, 2006) and *The Ark Builders* (Todmorden, UK: Arc Publications, 2009). In her poetry, O'Donnell ranges from fluid, inclusive reflections drawn from her South Ulster childhood roots, but also thematically explores the way we think about identity; specifically gender and national identity. Her range is both historical and contemporary, and she is conscious of what she calls the unlegendary heroic in the everyday. O'Donnell's first novel and best-seller, *The Lightmakers* (Dublin: Poolbeg Press, 1992), also addressed the complexities of female private and public realms, and the connections and clashes between the two, aspects that are reassessed in her critically praised modern morality tale *The Elysium Testament* (London: Trident Press, 1999). She is also the author of the novel *Virgin and the Boy* (Dublin: Poolbeg Press, 1996), and two collections of short fiction, *Strong Pagans* (Dublin: Poolbeg, 1991) and *Storm over Belfast* (Dublin: New Island, 2008). Interested in poetry relationships and other voices within Europe, during 2006 and 2007 she scripted, developed and presented the RTE national radio series 'Crossing the Lines'. This programme celebrated the newly accessed countries to the EU and introduced listeners to their poetry.

MANUELA PALACIOS is Associate Professor of English Literature at the University of Santiago de Compostela (Spain). She has directed several research projects on contemporary Irish and Galician women writers, which have been funded by the Spanish Ministry of Science and Innovation. She has co-edited three books on this topic: *Palabras extremas: Escritoras gallegas e irlandesas de hoy* (A Coruña: Netbiblo, 2008), *Writing Bonds: Irish and Galician Contemporary Women Poets* (Oxford: Peter Lang, 2009) and *Creation, Publishing, and Criticism: The Advance of Women's Writing* (New York: Peter Lang, 2010). Palacios has also edited and co-translated the bilingual anthology of Irish women poets *Pluriversos: Seis poetas irlandesas de hoxe* (Santiago: Follas Novas, 2003), and has translated contemporary European poetry and Virginia Woolf's fiction into Galician. She is the author of a number of critical studies on Irish literature which have appeared in *CLCWeb: Comparative Literature and Culture* (forthcoming), *European Journal of English Studies* 13.2 (2009), *Babel: Revue internationale de la traduction* 54.3 (2008), *Postcolonial and Gender Perspectives in Irish Studies* (2007), *Ireland in the Coming Time* (2006), *Feminismo/s* 5 (2005), *Gender, Sex and Translation* (2005), *Philologia Hispalensis* 17.2 (2003) and *Insights into Translation* (2003). Her other publications include monographs on Virginia Woolf's pictorial imagery (University of Santiago de Compostela, 1992) and Shakespeare's *Richard III* (Santiago: IGAEM, 2005).